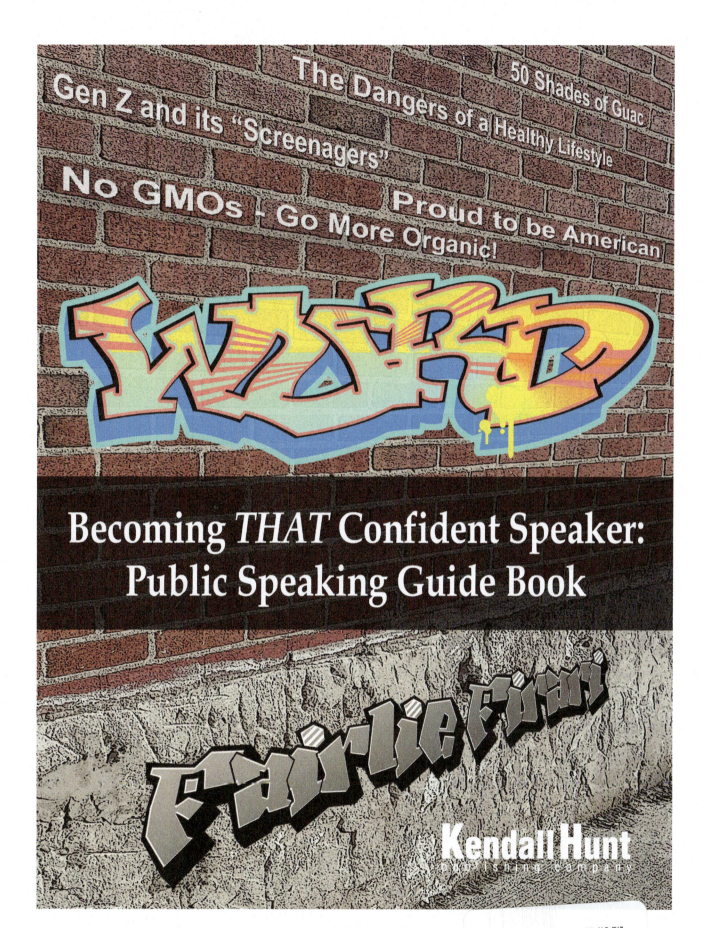

The Dangers of a Healthy Lifestyle

50 Shades of Guac

Gen Z and its "Screenagers"

No GMOs - Go More Organic!

Proud to be American

WORD

Becoming *THAT* Confident Speaker: Public Speaking Guide Book

FairlieFran

Kendall Hunt publishing company

D0024253

Cover design by Mohammed Suleiman

www.kendallhunt.com
Send all inquiries to:
4050 Westmark Drive
Dubuque, IA 52004-1840

Copyright © 2015 by Fairlie Firari

ISBN 978-1-4652-8690-1

Kendall Hunt Publishing Company has the exclusive rights to reproduce this work,
to prepare derivative works from this work, to publicly distribute this work,
to publicly perform this work and to publicly display this work.

All rights reserved. No part of this publication may be reproduced,
stored in a retrieval system, or transmitted, in any form or by any
means, electronic, mechanical, photocopying, recording, or otherwise,
without the prior written permission of the copyright owner.

Printed in the United States of America

CONTENTS

PREFACE

Textbooks are filled with valuable material but sometimes they contain more information than can be presented in one semester, especially for a performance-based class. With pressure on students to participate in extracurricular activities, sports, internships and often to hold jobs in addition to carrying a full academic workload it may be unrealistic to expect they will read 300 pages or more of four or five textbooks a semester. As an adjunct professor the choice made is usually between going long, trying to cover a lot of information, in hopes students will gain a cursory understanding of the material, or presenting less information and going deep so they will truly get to the core of a topic. Additionally with rapid advances in technology many textbooks need to be updated every couple of years, greatly devaluing these costly student purchases faster.

Also there has been a paradigm shift and to current generations the word "text" now means a short written exchange that is to the point and often seemingly somewhat cryptic because of a basic contextual understanding between the senders and receivers. The challenges of textbook length, cost, propensity to become outdated quickly and students' workloads plus a new definition of text begs an innovative approach to creating engaging and effective classroom materials.

In rethinking the approach to teaching public speaking or speech the first things considered were how to make the information relevant, to-the-point and skills based, and to increase student engagement by inspiring accountability for their own learning. It is interesting to learn that Aristotle was the father of rhetoric but 15-20 pages about his life does not help in speech preparation and delivery. Most students today know that for every speech there is a speaker, receivers, a message and a channel of communication. And this information though relevant does not need to be taught as a stand-alone lesson, it can be woven in where applicable. It also can be taught in a context more relatable to students for instance, each of these components are addressed by a hip-hop rapper in a one page article titled, *Ice T's 10 rules of public speaking* http://nypost.com/2012/06/10/ice-ts-10-rules-of-public-speaking/ where he succinctly addresses things like practicing and knowing the material, audience, and room.

This publication is designed to be either a workbook used in addition to a standard textbook or a stand-alone guide for minimalists who have their own materials and would like the students to, in effect, use it along with a journal where they can record their class activities and use again and again when they prepare to give other speeches and presentations. Its main purpose is to provide compulsory concepts using concisely written text, examples of current and future relevance, writing and speaking skill building assignments, and exercises requiring critical thinking.

This book is particularly unique because of the contributions made by the students. In this age of social media communication, peer-to-peer exchange is accepted and almost mandatory in some instances to establish street cred. This is a book for students created by those very actively involved with students and contains student contributions. The cartoons were created in collaboration with a former student of the author. It includes very apropos references and technologies, bringing public speaking from Ancient Greece to the 21st century in a manner that is very interactive and stimulating regardless of a student's learning style with a strong focus on performance and gaining much needed experience.

INTRODUCTION

How to Use This Guide Book

Fairlie Firari

Welcome to WORD! First you should know that according to the Urban Dictionary (2015) the word Word means "agreed" or "well said," so what better title for a publication on public speaking? Next you should meet the characters of the book who are for the most part based on the author and actual students, and represent actual incidents in and out of the classroom. They help illustrate the story of how to become a better public speaker.

The WORD Gang:

As individuals, the first character is Jon, a former student of the author and the artist who collaborated on the cartoon strips throughout this book. Jon taught me that individuals should defy categorization and be themselves.

The next character is Sierra, also a very gifted and awesome former student who is a writer, performer, and a person who will go very far in life. She has a message and is not afraid to speak it, especially in the form of her magnificent slam poetry. Sierra has taught me much about determination, the power of a smile, and intense, cut-right-through-you eye contact.

Next is Tiff, who is a combination of a few students and who is very focused on sports, has boundless energy, and has a huge heart. Tiff also has a love for animals and is a fiercely loyal friend. She is the teammate you want to have and takes everything to heart—always going the extra mile but sometimes she lets her self-doubt get in her way.

Then there is Hannah, also known as Hannah Guacamole, a former student who is bright and loves nothing more than food that is beautifully presented; she will probably own a restaurant someday but until then she will continue with her food blog and her work on fifty shades of guacamole. Hannah is not afraid to stand up for the underdog and will always champion what is fair and just!

Finally represented in cartoon form is the author, Dr. Firari, also known as Dr. F. She has been known to do some pretty outrageous things to keep her students engaged during class, including an impromptu speech demonstration on how to twerk (subject chosen by the class) in four different cultural styles. Where does she come up with those ideas!? She has a great passion for teaching many different communication classes.

DR. "F"

Since many students today either don't like to read much or just don't have the time, this book has little theory, lots of application and skills-based information, several visuals, practices, and is short and to the point.

This book is written to present the basics needed to understand what goes into writing and presenting excellent speeches and uses repetition to continually reinforce key points and instruction. You will also learn why some people have great anxiety about giving speeches and how to overcome the things that cause the anxiety or fears.

Each chapter will build onto the last chapter so that the book is progressive. You will first learn about the basic elements of a speech, then about the fear of public speaking, and then from chapter 3 on gain new techniques and skills to increase your abilities as a confident and credible presenter. At the end of each chapter are some questions and/or an activity to try, a reminder to make a journal entry, and a recommendation for an assignment, which will be described in an appendix at the back of the book but it will be up to your instructor to decide which assignment to give.

It is recommended that you keep a journal of what you are feeling and what you are learning, especially those "ah-ha" moments when something truly resonates with you and changes how you do something in preparing for or delivering a speech. For example, you may discover that you have a nervous habit of swaying back and forth that you didn't realize and you learned to stop. That's big! Perhaps you didn't know that including a good "attention getter" at the beginning of your speech can help pull the audience in and get them interested in your topic. You will find at the end of the semester that your journal is pretty full of new things that you've learned about yourself and others. This information will help you become a better communicator and even if you are not a Communication major, you will need to develop good communication skills for whatever profession you choose.

Please, keep an open mind about this class and make the conscious decision right now that you are going to succeed. Athletes do not go onto the field and start screaming for the medics at the mere sight of the opponent's size, nor do musicians go on stage thinking they don't need to bring their instrument because they are going to play so badly they might as well just leave it behind! NO, athletes and performers prepare, plan, and practice to be winners; and you will do the same thing in this class!! So get ready to tap your inner, winner public speaker—you will become THAT confident speaker, WORD?

Resources

Urban Dictionary. Retrieved June 11, 2015. http://www.urbandictionary.com/define.php?term=Word

CHAPTER 1

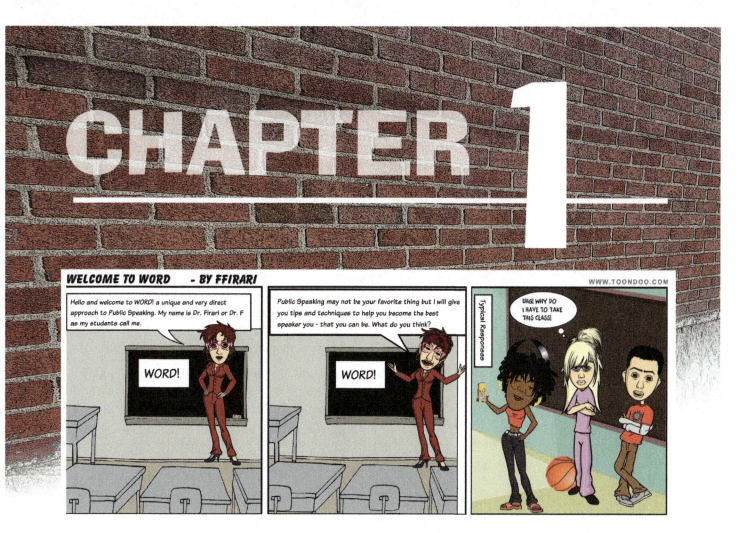

WHAT EVERY SPEAKER SHOULD KNOW

Fairlie Firari
Mark Meachem

Elements of a Speech

Some compare giving a speech to having a conversation, first pointing out the similarities (maybe this is to reduce anxiety); however, there are very big differences even though there are some of the same components to a speech and a conversation. For a conversation to take place, two or more people interact, they most likely know each other, and have a solid context for their discussion so the level of comfort during the exchange is high. During the conversation there is a potential for interruptions and also for the message to move quickly from topic to topic.

One type of conversation that *might* be compared to a speech would be a job interview. Here the level of anxiety is probably high, because the audience is usually more of an unknown entity. The interviewee or speaker is guarded, prepared and practiced, and hypersensitive to his or her surroundings, hoping it will end on a good note and looking forward to getting off the hot seat. For the interviewees, palms are sweaty, their voice may be a bit shaky, and they are worried about forgetting some of what they want to say and are trying to read the interviewer to figure how they are fairing. If you have ever given a speech you may be able to relate the feelings of going on an interview to the feelings you get when speaking publically.

Here are the biggest differences:

- A speech is given to an audience that may consist of many people the speaker has never seen before.
- The presentation is for the most part one sided; it is formal, focused and organized, sporting an introduction, main points, and a conclusion.
- The speaker may use a multimedia approach, stand behind a podium, and/ or hand out materials to the participants.

Another similarity between the two is the need for preparation. If you think about what it is you need to do before you go on an interview and then do many of the same things for a speech, you will have the correct mindset for public speaking.

For both you:

- Understand what is required to be successful.
- Study and research what you will be talking about.
- Investigate to the best of your ability to whom you will be speaking.
- Prepare questions to get more information.
- Plan how to put your best foot forward and appear credible.
  - o Prepare handout materials.
  - o Think about your greeting.
  - o Decide what to wear.
  - o Shower, brush your teeth, fix your hair, spit out your gum, and turn off your cellphone.
- Think about the room and what it might look like, to acclimate quickly.
- Practice what you will say and how you will look when you are speaking.
- Organize the most important points.
- Work on a solid closing that leaves the audience wanting more.

Now you have a reference point for the speech—think of it as similar to a job interview with more expansive elements. Below is a comprehensive list of the speech components followed by their individual definitions.

Components of a Speech

- Speaker
- Audience
- Topic
- Location
- Delivery method

- Time allotment
- Potential for feedback
- The unknown
- Noise/interference

The Speaker—in this case, is you. Whether the speech is a class assignment, a work-related presentation, or an entertaining discourse, the same approach to preparation, planning, practicing, and delivering is recommended. Because this is a guide book for college students, however, the focus will be on class assignment speeches.

First and foremost to be successful and to earn the *A*, you must learn to give the impression that you are confident (whether you are or not); learn how to quickly establish credibility and rapport with your audiences and overcome any anxiety or predisposed idea of failure. When you are confident and your audience is with you, you cannot fail!

The following sections of this manual are dedicated to providing the tools and guidance, amassed over twenty years, to assist you in building your most successful public speaker you. Chapter Two is dedicated to the subject of understanding the fear of public speaking reiterating the importance of establishing a mindset of success. A quick tip now though is to think about managing your self-talk. What are you saying to yourself before you give a speech? "I'm gonna start shaking as soon as I start talking," or "I know I'm going to forget what I want to say!" Seriously? Now that is not going to fly! Think of yourself as either an athlete stepping onto the field, court, or into the ring or a performer walking onto the stage—*now* what are you saying to yourself? "I got this!" "I've trained hard for this and I'm ready to kick some butt!" "Oh yea—this is mine." These are the same things you need to say to yourself before giving your presentation. Then shortly before it's your turn to speak take a few breaths of air—inhaling through the nose, exhaling slowly out through the mouth while visualizing your success. Then stand up, push your chest out, and walk to the front of the room like you own it—because you do.

A couple of other things to keep in mind are that many of the people in the audience, who you may think are intimidating, are usually very supportive mainly because they are happy it is you up there and not them. They know that you will be looking at them at some point when they have to speak, or are totally thinking about their own speeches and looking *toward* you but not really *at* you. So in reality, it is not that much about you; which for some of you will be good news.

The Audience—consists of the people sitting in the chairs in front of you with eyes riveted on your every move and their thoughts captivated by every word you speak. Or, more realistically for some of you, are the creepers that keep looking at you who you wish would just go away! If you are of the second mindset then we have some work to do because the audience can be your biggest ally and help you through this ordeal called P-U-B-L-I-C S-P-E-A-K-I-N-G!

Now here is some advice for students: Instead of entering the classroom and immediately engaging on your cellphone, talk to other students. What? I know! That is a crazy idea but here is the logic: When you get to know people in the class, the audience members for your speeches become more like friends than strangers and less intimidating. You will find out you have many things in common and share some of the same challenges and anxieties.

Professionals often "work a room" before giving a speech, introducing themselves to people, finding out a little about the folks in the room and what they are interested in learning, not so much because they are friendly but more because these speakers are trying to lower their anxiety by making a few friends in the audience. Expert presenters will then interact with some of these same audience members, perhaps calling them by name or engaging them with eye contact, all to make themselves and the audience feel more at ease. This is a great way to exude confidence and build rapport. Now where have we heard that before? Try it, put away the cellphone and engage face-to-face!

There is an entire section dedicated to audience analysis so for now keep in mind that without an audience there is no speech and if there is no speech then it is very hard to pass speech class, so they are critical. ***WORD?***

The Topic—this is obviously the subject of your verbal rhetoric (fancy way to say speech). The topic is central to your speech, to raising your level of confidence and ultimately your success. The topic selection first must be very interesting to you and sometimes even a passion of yours; second, this selection will be of interest to the audience, and finally will meet the criteria of the assignment. Selecting a good topic will be explored throughout this publication, including in Chapter Three. For now please keep in mind that there are lots of subjects to speak on and there are lots of subjects that have already been spoken on—*ad nauseum* (that is Latin for something that has gone on so long it makes you nauseous). Some of the overdone topics (please, give your speech professor a break) include:

- Legalizing Marijuana
- Driving and Texting
- Lowering the Drinking Age to 18
- Donating Blood
- Dangers of Smoking
- Dangers of Obesity
- Tanning Beds Cause Cancer
- Practicing Safe Sex
- The Importance of Exercising

Blah, blah, blah—come on now, is that the best you can come up with? You will find a few, more progressive and relevant ideas later on in this section. Don't just GOOGLE "Speech Topics" and select one because it sounds easy to speak about. Chances are a few other people in the class will do the same thing and then there will be four speeches on Organ Donation! What are you majoring in and what are the latest technologies or practices within that major that you can talk about? What is going on in the world, in sports, in entertainment in the health field, in a club that you belong to on campus that you can draw on for speech topics?

The Location—here we are talking about where the speech will be given; and this is very important because it is the environment where you must become familiar and comfortable so that you are not distracted. You will want to know how big the room is, the setup of the seating, where to focus while speaking, and how to place everything you need at your fingertips such as the computer, the remote slide changer or keyboard, the microphone if you need one, and the light switches in case you want to turn any lights down during part of your presentation for a video or bring lights up for other visuals. In essence you must become a part of your speech environment so you're assimilated rather than looking like a fish out of water.

Chances are you will be in a classroom that is already familiar to you, which may be one less thing to worry about. When you are giving a speech in a new space, however, it is a very good idea to get there early to have a good look around.

The Delivery Method—this is sometimes called the delivery channel and is the means by which the speech is actually given. In most cases for the classroom setting you will be using your voice as the delivery method.

Other delivery methods include webcasts, podcasts, television, radio, video, YouTube, and livestream. There may also be times when you are in a large facility (and you would know this because you scouted out the location in advance) where you will need to use a microphone, either one that is on a stand or perhaps a mic that travels. This is all very valuable information to get in advance.

The Time Allotment—simply speaking, this refers to how much time you have to give your speech. Most assignments are given with a specific time range, as are most professional presentations, for example 6-8 minutes. Staying within the allotted time is important to meet the assignment requirements, to make sure that the class does not get behind—which can easily happen if too many students go over the time limit—and to be respectful to other speakers waiting to present.

The best way to try to ensure that your timing is correct is to practice, although that may not be a sure bet because of what may happen once you get in front of the room. There is a weird phenomenon that happens to many people during a speech which can be likened to an **out-of-body experience**. Something strange happens physiologically and speakers are no longer aware of what they are saying, how they are saying it, what is happening with their voice or body, and whether time is standing still or speeding up. Students are surprised when they find out they have spent double the time allotted on their speech, often remarking that they experienced this out-of-body feeling which is a disconnect from their own sense of cognitive being or reality. For learning to control this effect, experience is the best remedy but videotaping and reviewing your speeches is also very helpful so that you can re-experience your performance once you are back in your body.

The Potential for Unsolicited Feedback or Reactions—is present from a variety of sources today, more so now than ever because of social media. We have become much more vulnerable or "viral-able" to warranted and unwarranted reactions. The same thing can happen during a speech but in different ways. Sometimes reactions look like a room full of bored college students, a few of whom are trying to sneak a peek at their cellphones on the down low and others who are practicing the art of sleeping with their eyes open. Other times unsolicited feedback is more encouraging and the class is engaged and students are responsive, giving lots of eye contact, smiling, and interacting.

When giving a speech it is important to establish eye contact with your participants in hopes of getting some back and to read your audience to make sure they seem to understand what you are saying and are following along. Confused or bored expressions are not good reactions and require you to change it up; eye contact, smiles, and nods are good reactions and let you know that all your preparations and practice are paying off! What is it you said to yourself before you started? Oh, "I got this!"

The Unknown—so basically you need to be ready with a Plan B just in case and you need to be able to think on your feet. What could possibly go wrong…?

- The computer equipment doesn't work.
- You can't open your presentation.
- The person who was supposed to go before you didn't show so you're up.
- You woke up sick but have to present.
- The person before you is doing the exact same topic.
- There are people in the room you don't know.
- There is a substitute teacher.
- The fire alarm goes off in the middle of your speech.
- Your cellphone keeps ringing but it's in your backpack at your desk and you are in the front of the room.

These are good times to use some critical thinking skills, which is discussed below.

Noise/Interference—can be caused by almost anything and is defined as something that interrupts the flow of a speech, distracts the audience, or prevents the audience from hearing or seeing the speaker or the visuals being presented. President Obama was just starting a speech once in the Rose Garden outside the White House and as he welcomed everyone, Air Force One flew overhead and the audience could see the president's lips moving but could only hear the sound of the planes. That was noise!

Noise can also be negative self-talk, resulting in increased fear and anxiety and the inability to deliver a speech confidently and credibly.

The Role of Critical Thinking

To deliver a well-developed presentation, it is important that you are also a skilled critical thinker. Your speaking skills and gestures can be excellent but if you have not designed a well-thought-out point to your speech, you won't persuade your audience at all. Logic and critical thinking are the elements in your speech preparation that will lead to your audience taking action. Think of it this way, perhaps you have eaten at a Teppanyaki restaurant, which is an Asian restaurant where they cook the food right in front of your table. The chef will do tricks, make colorful flames from the grill, make jokes, and generally impress you with culinary talents. All of that can be entertaining and exciting. However, no matter how much fun you have, if the food that the chef prepared tasted bad, you do not want to return to the restaurant and you will not tell others to go there. The same goes for a presentation you put together, no matter how much you captivate the audience with graphics, energy, and gestures, if you do not have a well-designed message for the audience to walk away with, your audience will not remember what you said or be motivated to try something new.

Critical thinking can have many definitions depending on the situations, and the varied meanings can create confusion. So, what do we mean by the term "critical thinking?" We tend to follow the definition created by former University of Illinois philosophy professor Robert H. Ennis (1995) who defined it as "reasonable reflective thinking that is focused on deciding what to believe or do." Emerging from this definition, Ennis (2002) listed ways to identify a critical thinker as the following:

A SUPER-STREAMLINED CONCEPTION OF CRITICAL THINKING

A critical thinker:
1. is open-minded and mindful of alternatives
2. desires to be, and is, well informed
3. judges well the credibility of sources
4. identifies reasons, assumptions, and conclusions
5. asks appropriate clarifying questions
6. judges well the quality of an argument, including its reasons, assumptions, evidence, and their degree of support for the conclusion
7. can well develop and defend a reasonable position regarding a belief or an action, doing justice to challenges
8. formulates plausible hypotheses
9. plans and conducts experiments well
10. defines terms in a way appropriate for the context
11. draws conclusions when warranted – but with caution
12. integrates all of the above aspects of critical thinking

Throughout this publication we will be placing specific critical thinking skills into three tiers. The first, and foundational, tier of critical thinking skills helps you prepare for your speech and relates to verbs such as *identify, compare, define,* and *differentiate*. Then we will move on and ask presenters to reach a second tier of critical thinking that builds upon the first tier. This next level helps you plan your speech and it relates to verbs such as *integrate, judge, examine, interpret, conclude,* and *connect*. Finally, we want students to reach the highest level of critical thinking. This level evolves only if you have practiced using the other two tiers of skills and you practice all that is suggested in this book. This tier involves terms such as *analyze, synthesize,* and *defend*.

Why Ethos, Pathos, and Logos Are Still Important

Aristotle (384–322 BC), the Father of Rhetoric, had it all right and his arguments are still valid today. According to Ramage and Bean (1998),

> The Greek philosopher Aristotle divided the means of [speaking] persuasion, appeals, into three categories—Ethos, Pathos, Logos. Ethos (Credibility), or ethical appeal, means convincing by the character of the author. We tend to believe people whom we respect. Pathos (Emotional) means persuading by appealing to the reader's emotions. We can look at texts ranging from classic essays to contemporary advertisements to see how pathos, emotional appeals, are used to persuade. Logos (Logical) means persuading by the use of reasoning.

President Obama is someone who has immediate cred (ethos) when he steps up to the podium whether it is in the Rose Garden or on the Edmund Pettus Bridge during the 50th anniversary of the Selma to Montgomery marches in 2015. By the very nature of his position as the president of the United States of America in addition to his ability to build rapport and establish trustworthiness, Barak Obama has ethos. President Obama also has an innate ability to vary between the effective use of pathos and logos.

When thinking about the makeup of an audience it is good to know that there are always people who will want to know what makes you the expert or wonder how much you really know about your topic so when ethos is established, those questions are answered. Within the audience are two other types, those who relate to emotions and those who relate to facts. Therefore, incorporating pathos and logos into most speeches along with projecting an expert persona or ethos is highly recommended.

Before we move on, let's really grasp the understanding of ethos, pathos, and logos. Below are YouTube links to some speeches. Identify three things you hear or see that indicate ethos or speaker credibility and/or trustworthiness. Does the speaker use pathos or statements that appeal to audience emotion and logos or facts and logic to make points? What do they say or do specifically to demonstrate ethos and logos?

Speech #1: This speech is, Malala Yousafzai Addressed United Nations Youth Assembly. It is 17:43 long and occurs on her 16th birthday. Yes, only 16 years old! The link is https://www.youtube.com/watch?v=3rNhZu3ttIU

EXAMPLES OF ETHOS:
(before you write in this book you may want to consider using pencil if you are thinking of reselling it, otherwise use your journal or a separate sheet of paper)

1)_____

2)_____

3)_____

EXAMPLES OF PATHOS:

1)_____

2)_____

3)_____

EXAMPLES OF LOGOS:

1)_____

2)_____

3)_____

Speech #2: Deonte Bridges, the first African-American male valedictorian in 10 years! Booker T. Washington High grad Deonte Bridges' Valedictorian speech, 4:58 long. The link is https://www.youtube.com/watch?v=Fwt4Byi8jRE

EXAMPLES OF ETHOS:

1)_____

2)_____

3)_____

EXAMPLES OF PATHOS:

1)_____

2)_____

3)_____

EXAMPLES OF LOGOS:

1)_____

2)_____

3)_____

Speech #3: Dusty Thompson talks about being true to yourself during the Funniest Leadership Speech ever! The link is https://www.youtube.com/watch?v=SA7b-Ko4HRTg

EXAMPLES OF ETHOS:

1)_____

2)_____

3)_____

EXAMPLES OF PATHOS:

1)_____

2)_____

3)_____

EXAMPLES OF LOGOS:

1)_____

2)_____

3)_____

There is one last topic to cover in this chapter and that is feedback. Feedback is different than criticism. Criticism sounds like, "You didn't speak loudly enough and I don't think you really practiced." The definition of criticism will usually contain words such as *disapproval*, *judgment*, or *faultfinding* so using the term *constructive criticism* must be an oxymoron, because what is positive faultfinding? A better term is **feedback** and it should be defined as "advice given based on an agreement to do so."

Managers, based on their role as supervisor, have a contractual responsibility to give feedback to employees regarding their performance, as determined by their job descriptions. That feedback should be specific, designed to help employees improve, and be delivered in an encouraging or neutral tone of voice. For example, "John, when you schedule morning meetings for 10:00 and then don't start them until 10:15, people start coming late knowing you won't start on time and we don't get as much accomplished because we have lost 15 or 20 minutes."

The same approach can be taken for a speech. The audience should give feedback based on goals set by the speaker and based on what is being taught in the class. It should be specific, designed to help the speaker perform better, and delivered in a neutral or encouraging tone of voice. Feedback does not sound like, "You did a really good job!" Why? Basically because that is not specific, meaning the speaker will not know what to do again the next time to get the same feedback. Feedback sounds like, "You met your goal to establish ethos when you told us you have been dancing since you were two years old and your eye contact could have been stronger because several times you looked at the floor instead of us."

For students it is highly recommended to practice properly giving AND receiving feedback because it is something you will be doing the rest of your academic and professional careers. At the beginning of each speech you should state one or two goals, based on prior teachings and/or weaknesses, that you hope to achieve during the speech. When the speech is over, you should first self-assess (how you think you did), then get peer feedback based on your goals, and then receive feedback from the instructor, which can be spoken or written—this author provides both.

As the person receiving the feedback you will simply say, "Thank you." You will not spend the next 2 or 3 minutes trying to explain why you did what you did or trying to explain what you meant to do, because first of all there is not enough time and second of all, no one cares. It will just end up sounding like a bunch of excuses! Sorry, just keeping it real here! Simply say, "Thank you" and then take the feedback if it will help you improve or ignore it if it will not.

Summary

Now let's take a quick look back at the highlights of this chapter. You learned about all the critical components of a speech and how they are defined; most of these will be examined in greater detail as we move forward.

You were introduced to the concept and applicability of critical thinking and its role in preparing, delivering, and evaluating your speeches. Critical thinking is a skill and therefore it can be developed and strengthened; it is also a lifelong tool for success.

Aristotle's ethos, pathos, and logos still have an important role in speech making, even after all these years. Sometimes you will want to focus mostly on logos because pathos may not be as imperative, say for an informational speech where the emphasis is on presenting the facts; however, establishing ethos in never optional, it is a requirement!

For those who do not love or perhaps even fear giving speeches you got some tips on how to project more confidence, you learned why that is important, and you know that more help for overcoming any fear or anxiety is on the way in Chapter Two! And finally, there was information presented about giving and receiving feedback.

Questions for You

1. What did you learn is the most important thing to do when preparing to give a speech, and how is this done?
2. What are some advantages to getting to know your audience prior to your speech?
3. Why is it important to project the image of an expert?
4. Name two speech delivery channels and explain what you would need to do differently to prepare for each.
5. If you only focused on two of the three Aristotelian means of speaking or persuasion, which would they be and why?
6. What is the difference between criticism and feedback?

Journal Entry:

Record your greatest learning for this chapter, what you think may be the most challenging and the easiest to accomplish. Then write some general thoughts and ideas for becoming THAT confident speaker.

Recommended assignment, Appendix A – Stand Up and Introduce Yourself

Resources

A Super-streamlined Conception of Critical Thinking. Retrieved June 11, 2015. http://orperhaps.blogspot.com/2010/11/defining-critical-thinking.html

Ennis, R.H. (1995) *Critical Thinking.* Upper Saddle River, NJ: Prentice Hall.

Ramage, John D., and John C. Bean. *Writing Arguments* (4th ed.). Needham Heights, MA: Allyn & Bacon, 1998, 81-82. Retrieved March 17, 2015. http://courses.durhamtech.edu/perkins/aris.html

WHAT ARE YOU AFRAID OF? GETTING AT THE ROOT CAUSE OF SPEAKERS' FEARS

Fairlie Firari
AnnMarie DiSiena

The Fears

Your name is called and it is your turn to speak. Uh oh! Here come the butter-flies, your heart starts to pound, your stomach churns, your palms get sweaty, you can't breathe, and you are thinking …nothing, crap, your mind just went completely blank! Great! Now what?

FEARS   - BY FFIRARI

The answer: Take a deep breath, in through the nose, hold, release slowly, exhale out through the mouth, smile, think positively, and do all the other things you will learn in this book that will help you become **THAT** confident speaker!

Speaking in public causes more anxiety than buying a house or divorce, and more fear than heights AND spiders! What you are experiencing is stage fright, a normal occurrence for most people. This same stage fright attacks athletes, dancers, actors, musicians, and others in the limelight.   Fear makes us feel stressed and yet it also produces the adrenaline that helps us perform well.

Think of a boxer who, before going into the ring, psyches him or herself out to perform well and win. This feeling is really an energetic response to get the adrenaline flowing and to do his or her best. The fear that we experience with public speaking is usually the fear of the unknown— the fear that we will not be successful or not perform well in front of others.

Steven Lucas (2004) tells us that fear of speaking even for experienced speakers ranks high on the anxiety list. He suggests that nervousness is a healthy sign and is a way of getting prepared for a positive outcome (Lucas, 2004). Shaky knees, quivering voice, inability to speak, and nausea are some of the symptoms of stage fright. Some people avoid public speaking because of these fears. Below are pictures of lists of fears expressed by students in the classroom and recorded on a blackboard during actual classes. Which ones do you identify with? Are there any missing? (Please excuse misspellings caused by trying to write too fast!)

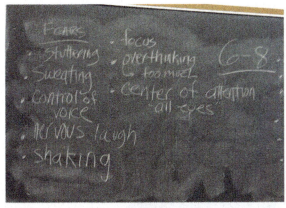
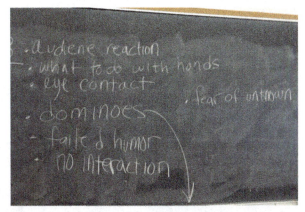

Class One
Fears

The second picture is a continuation of the first picture.
Dominoes means if one mistake is made during the speech then everything else will start to collapse.

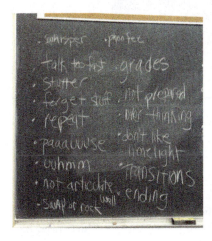
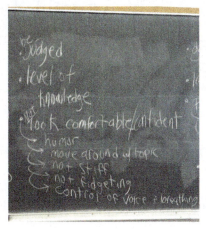
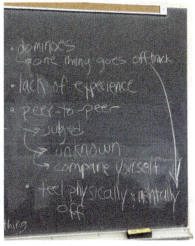

Class Two
Fears

The second and third pictures are continuations of the first picture.
"Phoofee" is a nonmedical way to say pass gas, which can happen when you are nervous.

Students consistently say they are afraid of being judged. Judged about:

- Appearance
- Ability to sound smart
- The topic they choose
- Any impediment they may have, like a stutter
- Ethnicity, religion, sexual orientation

Judging or stereotyping of any kind does not belong in the classroom, on the campus, or anywhere but sadly it exists. Please don't be a person who condones or perpetuates this kind of behavior; stereotyping needs to stop and it can end with us!

Also when you think about speaking in public, you may think about everybody taking notice of you and listening to what you have to say, and this is a good thing—not a bad thing. It is time to change your mindset about giving speeches because you have something to say and you have a voice! This book offers solutions to having a negative mindset, about being judged and other fears such as forgetting what you're going to say, level of knowledge, staying on track, not being prepared, making good transitions, and just about everything else listed in the blackboard pictures.

Anxiety is often caused by a lack of experience. Instead of speaking at every chance you get, you tend to shy away, avoid public speaking situations, and not take on the challenge (Dealing with Communication Anxiety and Public Speaking, n.d.). A college student may struggle through or avoid taking a required public speaking class until senior year as a result of the fear of speaking. You are not confident that you can do a good job or that you can be successful because you do not have a barometer or way to gauge your abilities, based on this lack of experience. The more often you practice speaking, the more automatic it becomes and the more confident you become in your abilities to give speeches (Beebe & Beebe, 2001; Lucas, 2004; Seiler & Beall, 2002). Overcoming the fear of public speaking is not easy, but it is achievable. Seiler and Beall (2002) indicate there are no complete cures for speech anxiety; they are only ways to reduce, manage, or control it. Identifying fears as normal, encouraging speaking, discussing the aspects of positive self-talk, and establishing a welcoming environment are some of the skills approaches to helping reduce the fear of speaking (Robinson II, 1997).

Think about it, what could happen? You might make a mistake but who will know? If this occurs, don't tell the audience you made a mistake—just keep going. The chance that your audience will know you made a mistake if you don't tell them is small AND it is only a mistake because you did or did not do something the way you had planned, so is it really a mistake if no one else knows? This is one of the good things about public speaking; you deliver a speech that comes from your thoughts. Yes, research is important and practice is necessary to deliver the content, but the thoughts are yours.

The Tools to Diminish the Fears

You will find in forthcoming chapters information on how to:

- **Prepare, Plan, Practice**—critical to feeling confident and establishing ethos. Following these guidelines will help overcome many of the above stated fears.
- **Use STATT**—this an outline format which is the basis for all speech types presented in this book, it will help you and the audience stay on track and help you remember what you want to say and when you want to say it, among other useful things.
- **Create Fantastic Slideshows**—this will help the visual learners in your audience, support your message with slides and take some of the attention off of you. So for those of you who don't like being in the limelight or having people stare at you, here is part of the solution.
- **Dress for Success**—wearing the appropriate outfit on speech day will help those of you who worry about being judged because of your appearance. You will get some great tips in following chapters.
- **Put on the Proper Mindset**—which is that of a winner. Change your self-talk from, "I can't do this and I'm going to screw-up" to "I CAN do this; I've got the pow-ah!"
- **Watch Your Language**—body and vocals, that is! There is an entire chapter devoted to how best to stand, move, what to do with your hands, feet, face, and eyes, and about vocals. When you look good and sound good and are not doing distracting things, then more focus is on the message and less focus is on the messenger plus you will again feel and look confident and credible.
- **Analyze, Listen, Respond to Your Audience**—knowing who your audience is and the audience's level of understanding of your topic, learning to listen and respond correctly to people and what they are saying, shows you are confident, builds rapport, and establishes you as a skilled speaker.

Cred or Crud? Becoming a Mini Subject Matter Expert

One other skill that is extremely important is to learn to become a subject matter expert (SME) on the topic you are presenting. It is not enough to simply speak about something you are familiar with, you must research and write about the subject so that the information in your speech is verifiable and adds cred and not crud to your content. Become a SME and you will definitely be able to manage several fears.

Written Plan for Overcoming Fears

This is a good time to get in touch with what really makes you nervous about public speaking, if you get nervous. It is not enough to know that public speaking causes you anxiety; knowing what specifically causes the anxiety is what is critical so that you can take steps to control and manage your fears. So carefully review what other students have said and what was recorded on the blackboard and what is written in this chapter or do some of your own additional research, then start creating a plan for what you are going to do to mitigate and manage your specific fears. Feel free to read ahead in this book if you think there is something mentioned in the tools list above that will help you. You will see that everything is outlined in the Table of Contents.

Journal

Your plan for overcoming your fears should be a work-in-progress and ever evolving. It is a good idea that your plan be written in a journal where you record other information about your public speaking journey, which will include such things as your goals for your speeches, assignment due dates, successes, need-to-improves, things other students did that you liked, notes from lectures that will help you improve your speaking, links to websites with good information, names of good speakers or speeches that you see, and anything else you want to make note of during the semester.

You can also use the journal to help you plan for upcoming speeches—topic ideas, resources to become a SME, a timeline to complete everything before the speech due date—leaving time to practice and setting up a practice schedule.

Summary

The fear of public speaking is real and in severe cases it is called glossophobia. The good news is, there are tools, techniques, and tips that will help everyone, minimally, get through this class and hopefully also unearth some true talent that will encourage others to pursue careers where public speaking is a regular experience. There have been no known reported severe injuries or deaths caused by giving speeches, so you can put that fear to rest and keep in mind that most people in the audience are very supportive! Now let's see what lies ahead.

Questions for You

1. The fear of public speaking is real but very personal. What do you think your greatest fear(s) might be and why? BE SPECIFIC!
2. What have you read so far that will help you overcome your fear(s)?
3. Go online and find five famous people who have a fear of public speaking and write about why you are surprised about each person and explain how each one has worked to overcome their fears.
4. Explain how the terms *mindset* and *self-talk* are related? How do they influence a speaker's performance?
5. Does knowing that the fear of public speaking is a real phenomenon help you or make things worse for you as a speaker and why?

Journal Entry:

Record your greatest learning for this chapter, what you think may be the most challenging and the easiest to accomplish. Then write some general thoughts and ideas for becoming THAT confident speaker. Go back and reread old entries. Were your challenges and accomplishments correct, if not what did you predict incorrectly that surprised you? Are some things harder or easier than originally thought?

Recommended Assignment, Appendix B – Demonstration Presentation

References

Beebe, S.A., S.J. Beebe, and D.K. Ivy. (2001). *Communication Principles for a Lifetime*. Boston: Allyn and Bacon.

Dealing with Communication Anxiety and Public Speaking. Retrieved February 3, 2004. Rochester Community and Technical College. http://www.roch.edu/dept/spchcom/anxiety_handout.htm

Lucas, S.E. (2004). *The Art of Public Speaking* (8th ed.). New York: McGraw Hill.

Robinson II, T.E. (DATE). Communication Apprehension and the Basic Speaking Course: A National Survey of In-class Treatment Techniques. *Communication Education*, 46(3), 188-197.

CHAPTER 3

WHO ARE YOU TALKING TO AND WHAT ARE YOU SAYING?

Fairlie Firari
Mark Meachem

Student Speech

Before diving into this chapter you will read a speech given by a student who took a Public Speaking class taught by this author. The point of including it is to show you how incorporating the information from this guide into speech writing and speaking, and in giving and receiving feedback, will help you gain confidence and improve your skills. Use and trust the techniques and processes described to build maximum self-assurance, establish credibility with audiences, and create and maintain interest in your speeches.

Student Entertainment Speech, written by Dan Trapanotto, 2015

Hi, I'm Daniel Trapanotto and today I'm going to be giving out an award for best professor. Quick show of hands, who here was afraid to take Public Speaking this semester. I'm glad we're on the same page because I was also very hesitant to take Public Speaking this semester. I had an awful time slot during registration so I usually pick last. There was no coincidence that Public Speaking was available since students tend to push that course off for another time. I decided to take it even though I was very nervous about it. Public Speaking was never one of my strong traits. I usually would start to shake and often blank about what I was going to say next. When I walked into this classroom on the first day I saw a bunch of unfamiliar faces and a professor with red hair. I thought to myself there was no way I was going to make it through the semester alive. On that very day we had to answer four simple questions while being videotaped. And I remember myself getting all worked up and nervous for that. I thought this class was going to be torture from here on out. But these thoughts slowly vanished from the help of this one professor. This professor taught us the power of STATT and the 3Ps (prepare, plan and practice). She made us, as a class, make a list of the things that scare us the most about Public Speaking. She broke down the list and showed us that Public Speaking isn't as bad as we make it out to be. She taught us proper body language and stance. So as the semester went on things got easier. Although the speeches got longer in length they became easier to cope with. By following STATT and 3Ps I felt I could get through anything. I've covered topics from demonstrating a dumbbell bench press using two water bottles, to persuading individuals against hazing. If you were to tell me that I had to do an impromptu speech in the beginning of the semester I would have quickly declined and not even attempted it. But instead, I kept my cool and talked about a mechanical beaver for about a minute or so. It was also very entertaining to see what everyone else could think of on the spot. Even when I thought I bombed a speech, this professor had nothing but positive things to say [power of feedback]. This goes for my classmates as well. I thank you guys for not ripping me apart whenever I finished a speech. Lastly, this professor helped us get through one of the most nerve wracking courses and she helped us do it together. We came together as a class and took this course one step at a time. You helped me face my fears and I can't thank you enough for that.

Audience Analysis

Without an audience there is no need to give a speech, so let's review the importance of audience analysis. To get information about your audience there are a few things you can do, but first let's explore why, from the speaker's perspective, this is helpful. Knowing a little about your audience lowers anxiety just because some familiarity is less stressful than none and you can identify people who will apt to be more friendly and receptive to you when you are speaking. This will also allow you to tailor the speech to the interest and knowledge level of the majority of the participants, leading to increased buy-in and interest.

Analysis is an area where the first level of critical thinking skills becomes important for the speaker. Identify who your audience is (conduct an analysis of your demographics, background knowledge of the topic, etc.). Are there more men or women in the audience? What is the general age of the audience? Is there a common geographic area they are from? Does the audience tend to hold certain general beliefs (religious, political, etc.)? Presenters must ask themselves questions about the people to whom they are speaking. Do not underestimate the importance of knowing the demographics of your audience. The information from examining the demographics should help you to know the best way to organize your presentation.

Exercise:

Let's imagine you are giving a presentation at a religious-affiliated college about sexual assaults on college campuses. Even if your facts and data remain the same, how will you adjust your content and focus to best connect with the audience?

Audience 1: 80% female, 20% male. 90% between the ages of 18 and 22. All enrolled in college. All social media savvy.

Audience 2: 70% male, 30% female. 75% between the ages of 45 and 60. 65% parents of college-aged children; 25% parents of children in high school; 10% have no children.

Audience 3: 80% college administrators/faculty/staff; 65% are older than 60 years; 15% are members of a religious order; 50% male, 50% female.

Before starting your speech, talk to people in the audience to find out what they know about your topic and to start building rapport and trust. This is where putting away the cellphone and having a live conversation is beneficial. Professional speakers will gather information about the audience from the event planners and will talk to people as they come into the room.

When you give a speech it is not as much for *you* as it is for ***them***. One thing many speakers forget is that a speech is given for the edification of the audience, not the glorification of the speaker! Dr. Martin Luther King Jr. did not give his "I Have a Dream" speech so that people would admire him, but rather so that African-Americans would have a voice and to send a message to Americans of all races. You can watch that speech at www.youtube.com/watch?v=smEqnnklfYs Keep in mind that the type of speech Dr. King made in 1963 was on a much grander scale than what is being talked about in this publication; however, you should still consider establishing ethos (trustworthiness and credibility) and using pathos (passion) and logos

CHAPTER THREE: Who Are You Talking To And What Are You Saying?

25

(logic) to meet the needs of the audience, which you can do best once you've done the analysis.

One student learned a very hard lesson in a class recently when he thought it would be funny to compare the advantages to drinking beer over spending time with women, using a scoring system where women came in second place. Now first of all, the topic itself is inappropriate; and second, audience analysis was not conducted because the majority of the audience was female. This event is discussed further under the heading of Respect, Integrity, and Ethics.

Now part two of analyzing your audience requires setting a comfortable tone, and getting to know a little bit more about the participants' level of knowledge of your topic right at the beginning of your speech, in hopes of keeping them engaged and interested. If the majority of the group knows a lot on the topic, then you can speak to a higher level; but if not, then starting with a longer introduction or giving more information on the topic basics/background or origin would be important.

At the start of your speech it is good to poll the audience to find out how much they know about your topic by asking questions such as:

- How many of you have heard of the Tough Mudder? Has anyone actually run the Tough Mudder or known someone who has and lived!?
- With a show of hands, have you ever suffered from or been the victim of road range?
- How many of you have rescued a dog or dogs from a shelter?

Asking these types of closed-ended questions will give you an understanding of who/how many in the audience are familiar with your topic and at what level, and who is not familiar. It will also let the participants know who they have something in common with and the questions can be used as great **attention getters** (we'll discuss these more later), while moving everyone on to the same page.

Professionals giving long workshops will do all the things above and will also let people know where the bathrooms are, when breaks and lunch are scheduled, and other details such as when it is appropriate to ask questions, for example, is during the session okay or should they be held for the end. This is done so everyone knows what to expect and sets a positive and comfortable atmosphere in the room. When your audience is comfortable they will give off an encouraging vibe, which will in-turn help you feel less anxious.

POP QUIZ

If you do not analyze your audience you risk…? Select the right answer:

A. Boring them because they have a higher level of knowledge than what you are presenting
B. Boring them because you are speaking about something of which they have no knowledge and you are speaking at too high a level of knowledge
C. Boring them because they are not at all interested in what you are speaking about
D. Alienating your audience because you did not figure out a way to build rapport and establish credibility or trustworthiness
E. A, B, D
F. All of the above

The answer written in American Sign Language: . Did you pass the quiz?

Africa Studio/Shutterstock

Content, Becoming a Mini SME through Research

In preparing the speech content, clearly define the main points of your presentation to support your goal of informing, influencing, or entertaining the audience. Think about what result you want. An effective speaker must identify how best to reach the audience by making the message relatable. The best place to start is with research, research, research. Professionals are asked to speak about topics on which they are subject matter experts (SMEs, pronounced smee); therefore, you must become a mini SME. Research your topic to gather the information you need to support your speech with facts, to establish credibility or ethos and to sound confident when you are speaking. This is how to "bring it," especially for those of you whose public speaking fears include not knowing what to speak about or not having enough information.

It is suggested to write a one- to two-page research paper as discussed in the section on the 3Ps. Not only is it good to learn how to conduct research and hone fact gathering skills, but also the information will be the foundation of your presentation—which you can build on and which will provide logic/facts or logos.

So through research we have ethos and logos covered, now what about pathos? Pathos is an appeal to the emotions of the audience and evokes sympathy, empathy, happiness, sadness, fear, or anger but is still based on facts; therefore, the research is critical to establish ethos, logos, AND pathos. For example, according to CNN (2015) more than 8,000 people died in the Nepal earthquake in May 2015, including many children and elderly. Remember your audience is made up of some people who relate more to logic and facts (over 8,000), some who relate more to emotion (children and elderly), and all who expect the truth. Add a video or some pictures of the horrors of the earthquake and you will have a commanding presentation about the powerful effects of natural disasters. This is what research and becoming a SME is all about.

CHAPTER THREE: Who Are You Talking To And What Are You Saying?

27

Respect, Integrity, and Ethics

RESPECT

Respect the audience and respect the speaker. Let's look at the example from earlier about the speech titled, *Beer versus Women*, to really emphasize the point that making women or any gender, race, ethnicity, religion, sexual orientation, or belief the target of a speech is not acceptable, especially when the majority of the class is of one of those groups and is left to feel objectified, devalued, and disrespected. And then to have the speaker and other male students compound the problem by stating that the feelings of the female students were "stupid" for not receiving the speech as a joke is a further lack of respect and sadly endemic of a greater problem on college campuses which can't be addressed here. Be aware that actions have consequences and actions will garner reactions.

PRESENTATION GONE WRONG   – BY FFIRARI

As a speaker you cannot control the reaction of others but you can control what others are reacting to, so try to *give* respect in hopes you will *get* respect. Sadly the current most popular definition of respect in the Urban Dictionary written by Anonymous is, "A quality seriously lacking in today's society" (2015). Thankfully there is another definition written by Peppermint Rose that is more uplifting and is the second most popular in the Urban Dictionary: "It means valuing each other's points of views. It means being open to being wrong. It means accepting people as they are. It means not dumping on someone because you're having a bad day. It means being polite and kind always, because being kind to people is not negotiable. It means not dissing people because they're different to you. It means not gossiping about people or spreading lies" (2015). What is key in the second definition is that if we are accepting of and value others, are polite and kind and don't dis people, then chances are we are respectful! Respect means we are truthful, honest, and we do not violate, harm, destroy, or defame someone else or their possessions. So what do you think about a topic titled, *Beer versus Women*? Respectful? Appropriate for an audience primarily of women? Funny? Harmless?

INTEGRITY AND ETHICS

So what is the difference between integrity and ethics? Integrity is knowing and doing the right thing motivated by internal feelings; ethics are externally driven and are about following rules, procedures, and beliefs. High integrity says to turn in the found wallet with all the money still inside because someone is hurting without their cash and ID and ethics says turn in the wallet with all the money inside because getting caught with it could get you in big trouble.

While respect is more related to how the audience and speaker are treated, writing a speech that gives full credit to the proper sources for material that is not original shows integrity and is ethical. Plagiarism, or using someone else's work, in any form is unethical and it is very easy to catch. It is advisable to read the plagiarism guidelines for your school to find out the consequences because if plagiarizing doesn't concern you from an integrity standpoint it may concern you from an ethics standpoint. Plagiarism, in some instances, can get you expelled from school.

You must give credit to your sources and it starts with the research paper. Once you've written the paper you should have a list of all your citations so giving credit within the speech is not difficult. In fact when you mention sources during a presentation then your credibility increases. For example, in a presentation on virtual reality games you might say something like, "According to Jack Smith IV, a writer for mic.com, 'One million people around you [right now] are playing an alternate-reality game you can't see' (2015) and the game is Ingress." It is as simple as mentioning Jack Smith IV of mic.com or the AMA or ASPCA—depending on your topic and your sources. When you subtly add the name of some of your sources to your speech you increase the legitimacy of what you are saying and of your own credibility. So for those of you whose fear is looking stupid, this is part of the cure for you.

CHAPTER THREE: Who Are You Talking To And What Are You Saying?

29

Speech Format—STATT

Many students over the years have expressed their fear of forgetting what they were going to say. Following a tried and true format as the base for almost every type of speech will help remedy that and is a good idea for many reasons. The one recommended here was partially developed by students and has earned the acronym S-T-A-T-T as an easy way to remember the speech elements.

[S] The first S in S-T-A-T-T stands for "self-introduction." Before starting any speech it is a good idea to introduce yourself and in some cases to say a little about why you are there. For example, *"Good afternoon, my name is Sierra and I'm going to do a little performance for you today."*

[T] Next comes the first T—the topic introduction or "tell 'em what you're going to tell 'em." Here you will let the audience know what your speech is about, just like you do when writing your paper and you introduce the subject. In staying with the example of Sierra, she might say something next like, *"Writing and performing poetry is a great*

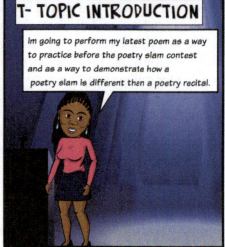

artistic outlet and I have entered the slam competition happening tomorrow night so for this speech I'm going to perform my latest poem as a way to practice before the contest and as a way to demonstrate how a poetry slam is different than a poetry recital."

[A] Earlier I mentioned including an **attention getter** so here is a good place for one. Sometimes speakers will actually start their speech with an attention getter and that is perfectly fine. The attention getter is exactly what it sounds like and is used to pull your audience in and get them started thinking about what you are going to talk about next in the speech. For many students using a polling question or two as the attention getter is a good way to break the ice and conduct audience analysis at the same time. Sierra might then say, *"I have been performing my original poems here at school for the last two years and last year I won 1ˢᵗ place in the women's and overall categories (cred!), so how many of you know the difference between a poetry recital and a poetry slam? And how many of you have been to the poetry slams here?*

[T] The next T stands for "tell 'em" and includes the actual speech, the majority of which is drawn from the research and should be organized in a similar style or format as the paper with two or three main points, each having two or three sub-points, and so on, depending on how in-depth the topic is and how much time is allotted for the speech.

Example Topic:

Trimming a Dog's Nails

- Types of Nails
  - Black
  - Clear
  - Brown/tan
- Tools and Supplies
  - Nail cutters
  - Leashes or restraints
  - Powder to stop bleeding
  - Towels and broom
- How to Handle the Dog
  - Holding positions
  - Having an assistant
  - Types of reactions
    - Growling and snapping
    - Shaking and whining
    - Signs to stop and let go

[T] And the final T stands for "tell 'em what you told 'em" and this is the conclusion, again just like you would have in the research paper. For some reason student speakers often drop the ball here and do not finish with a bang but rather with a whimper that sounds something like, "Yea, okay well that's my speech." WHAT! After all that work that is your conclusion? In the example of Sierra it should sound something like, *"And THAT is how you slam poetry, you have to demonstrate the power and emotions of the words and phrases through the use of your voice and your whole body, in particular through your eyes, rather than simply reading or reciting. I hope you learned something new and enjoyed my performance. Don't forget tomorrow night at 7:00; there will be lots of refreshments. Thank you."* Now that is a conclusion. Wrap up the speech with a nice bow as part of a complete "present" - ation! Get it, bow - present? That's a little speech humor!

The STATT format will help you stay organized and focused. You can use it for almost any presentation.

S elf-introduction
T ell 'em what you're going to tell 'em
A ttention getter
T ell 'em
T ell 'em what you told 'em

The 3Ps: Prepare, Plan, and Practice

It is very important when speaking publicly to adopt the 3P process: Prepare, Plan, and Practice. Practice is especially important, to avoid that out-of-body phenomenon mentioned earlier, where you seem to float above yourself and watch what is happening as if you have no control and then when the speech is over, you also have no memory of how you did or what you said! Preparing, planning, and practicing will help make sure that you are still doing a good job even though you may go out-of-body!

Preparing requires selecting and researching an interesting topic, outlining the speech, and preparing notecards or, even better, a PowerPoint or Prezi presentation. Selecting a good topic is done based on your interests, the interests and level of knowledge of the audience, and of course the requirements of the assignment.

Topics should be relevant to the audience—in other words, a speech to a class that is predominately upper classmen about *How to Get Through Your Freshman Year* **is not** relevant, but a speech on *How to Get the Internship You Really Want* **is** relevant. The subject must also be of interest to the speaker. Trying to research and speak on a topic that is not interesting to you will result in you getting bored, most likely the audience getting bored, and perhaps a not so good grade. There are so many options that interest students that thinking creatively will pay off.

SELECTING TOPIC   - BY FFIRARI

What is not interesting is an informative speech about cigarette smoking causing cancer—that's been done, it is not new news, and in fact the public is inundated with commercials on television of people with cancer talking to and showing us things we would rather not see, such as holes in the throat or a son bathing his bedridden mother, so don't go there.

Examples of interesting informative topics could include:

- The Origin and Resurgence of Barbie
- Benefits to Chewing Bubble Gum
- Increase and Infiltration of GMOs into Our Food
- Islam versus Radical Islam
- The Benefits of Studying Abroad
- Concussions and Second Concussions
- Batman
- Reducing Stress at College
- Gen Z and Its 'Screenagers'
- Restorative Justice in Public Schools Back Fires
- Ingress – Alternate Reality

With GOOGLE, Yahoo, YouTube, and other Internet resources it is very easy to explore for and find topics.

Also as part of **preparing**, it is recommended that for each major speech assignment, you write a research paper. This paper is true research and not an explanation of what is going to be presented. It will contain an introduction, body, conclusion, a minimum of three valid citations, and be up to three pages long. There is no better way to become well versed on a topic than to study and write about it enough to become a mini SME. As mentioned earlier, in the professional world those called upon to do presentations and speeches are those known as SMEs within their fields. Becoming a SME on the topic being presented will increase your confidence and credibility. Hmmmm, seems like we heard about SMEs, confidence and credibility somewhere before, perhaps on more than one occasion!

Research Paper Introduction

The research paper introduction will introduce the topic to the reader and set the stage for what will be accomplished in the rest of essay. This should not be new to you as college students; you know it is important to create the correct expectations for the readers. It is here where you *tell them what you are going to tell them* and entice them into reading more.

Research Paper Body

Next comes the meat of the paper or the body and here is where *you tell them*. The bulk of your research makes up the body of the text; it contains interesting facts about things the readers might not know and sometimes differing points of views. This writing is of course properly cited to give credit where credit is due, to avoid plagiarism of any type and to validate the information being presented in the paper with multiple resources.

RESEARCH PAPER CONCLUSION

To wrap up the paper, the written conclusion *tells them what you told them.* Without a strong conclusion the writing will fall short and flat.

Here is an example of the requirements of a research paper. Say your research topic is on:

The Consequences of Mixing Adderall with Alcohol

The introduction will present the subject and talk about what will be included in the paper, such as information about what type of drug Adderall is and its pros and cons.

The body of the speech will go into great detail about the drug as described in the introduction.

I.   Description of Adderall
    a. Type of drug – prescription or over-the-counter
    b. How Adderall is taken

II.   Pros of Adderall
    a. What Adderall is designed to treat
    b. If it can be used for other symptoms

III.   Cons of Adderall
    a. Side effects and addiction
    b. Dangers of abusing and mixing with alcohol

In the conclusion, just like with a conversation, there should be a good-bye for each hello! For this topic the writer would conclude by reiterating that Adderall is a drug for treating specific symptoms and has many good qualities but should only be taken as prescribed and never mixed with alcohol use.

Let's look at citations for a moment as valuable tools to writing a credible paper. First, no Wikipedia, because information from this source is not reliable given it is an open forum where anyone can contribute. You should include information from viable sources such as academic or industry SMEs within your text for support and substantiation. Again, this will increase your credibility by providing proof of evidence.

You will see in later sections how this approach of intro, body, conclusion, and proper use of citations is also very relevant to speech preparation, so remember what is written here and be encouraged to refer back when building your speeches.

PLANNING

Examining the speech venue and identifying what you will need to effectively deliver a speech is very important. You should become familiar with the room where you are speaking and answer the following questions:

- What equipment do I need and is it provided?
- Should I have handouts and how many?
- Are there physical constraints at the venue; is it small or large, noisy, do people pass in front of me to get to their seats…etc.?
- What is the best way to grab the attention of the audience?
- Should I use visual aids to add interest and promote better understanding?
- Do I have a backup plan in case the equipment doesn't work?
- Should I bring a USB with my presentation slides on it?
- What should I wear?
- Do I have a bottle of water?

PRACTICING

People often say that practice makes perfect; however, in reality it makes things really, really good, because perfection doesn't exist and it is something that puts too much pressure on people to achieve! Check out Jan Brewer on YouTube, a seasoned speaker and politician who Made Larry, Barry and Terry Very Uncomfortable (https://www.youtube.com/watch?v=xH-MbrQY15o). Oh well, she slipped up, she was not perfect, but was she reelected? YES!

Speeches last only a few minutes and mistakes are but a few moments in time within those speeches, usually without lasting consequences. As was mentioned in an earlier chapter about making a mistake during a speech, unless it is pretty obvious, the only way the audience knows when you make a mistake is when you confess! "Crap, I meant to say…" or "Shoot, I was going to… ." Why are you confessing? Don't tell your audience when you screw up, either with words or with body language and they will never know. In reality it is only a screw-up because you didn't say something exactly the way you wanted to say it, so what is the big deal?

If you have truly **prepared, planned, practiced**, done the research and have become a mini **SME**, polled the audience, and are following **STATT,** then you cannot go far off course! So practice. Practice with friends, family, in front of the mirror, with your iPhone recording your audio or video, and keep running the key thoughts or points over and over in your head so when it comes time to speak everything comes together and rolls out more easily than you even imagined.

In the next chapter you will kick it up even one more level, so by the time you reach the end of this guide you will be *THAT* confident speaker. WORD!

Questions for You

1. Why is audience analysis conducted before **and** during a speech? How is it best done before and how is it done during?
2. What is a SME and how can you become one?
3. Write about a time when you exhibited respect or integrity or took an ethical stance.
4. What do you find the most helpful about having the STATT format as guidance?
5. Which of the three Ps do you think you can skip if you are pressed for time? Why do you think you can skip that one?

Activity

Preparing, planning, and practicing take time but are vital to your success as a speaker. Think about and record in your journal some ways you can actually make room in your busy schedule or ways to reprioritize to make time for the 3Ps. You know what assignments are coming up and when they are due and you know what else you have on your schedule. What can you do proactively to ensure you aren't scrambling at the last minute to get ready, which will only make you more nervous and you know that it never works out either?

Journal Entry:

Record your greatest learning for this chapter, what you think may be the most challenging and the easiest to accomplish. Then write some general thoughts and ideas for becoming THAT confident speaker. Go back and reread old entries. Were your challenges and accomplishments correct, if not what did you predict incorrectly that surprised you? Are some things harder or easier than originally thought?

Recommend Assignment – Research Paper for Informative Speech

Resources

Death Toll in Nepal Earthquake Tops 8,000. Retrieved June, 11, 2015. CNN. http://www.cnn.com/2015/05/10/asia/nepal-earthquake-death-toll/

Millions of People Around You Are Playing an Alternate Reality Game You Can't See. Retrieved June 11, 2015. Tech.Mic. http://mic.com/articles/119366/one-million-people-around-you-are-playing-an-alternate-reality-game-you-can-t-see

Urban Dictionary by Anonymous. Retrieved May 28, 2015. http://www.urbandictionary.com/define.php?term=respect

Urban Dictionary by Peppermint Rose. Retrieved May 28, 2015. http://www.urbandictionary.com/define.php?term=respect

CHAPTER THREE: Who Are You Talking To And What Are You Saying?

37

WHAT DO YOU SOUND AND LOOK LIKE WHEN YOU ARE SPEAKING?

Fairlie Firari

There has been a lot of information so far in this guide about the content, so now it is time to discuss vocals and body language. First, however, let's put the three—content, vocals, and body language—in perspective by looking at the percent of impact or influence they each have on the audience.

Three influences:	Three percentages:
Content	55%
Vocals – how you say things/tone of voice	38%
Body language	7%

Which influence belongs with which percentage? Is it:

A. Content 38% Vocals 55% Body language 7%
B. Content 55% Vocals 7% Body language 38%
C. Content 7% Vocals 38% Body language 55%
D. Content 55% Vocals 38% Body language 7%

The answer is C unless the speaker is really, really good; then the answer is D. What? That is confusing!

Statistics say the answer is C, that only 7% of content or what is said is impacting the audience, but how the voice sounds impacts the audience by 38% and what the body is doing during the speech influences the audience and its ability to focus on the message by 55%. In other words your voice and body can actually distract from the speech—UNLESS your vocals and body language are really, really good. Many speakers, however, have strange vocal and body language behaviors that they are often not aware of but can easily correct with some good tips, feedback, and practice.

Chart 1 shows the differences between what statistics describe as the percentages applied to the influences of content, vocals and body language on the audience. Chart 2 shows percentages as applied to what this book deems to be a really, really good speaker.

Table 1 shows the characteristics of a 55% body language speaker vs. a 7% really, really good speaker.

CHART 1. Typical Speaker

CHART 2. Really, Really Good Speaker

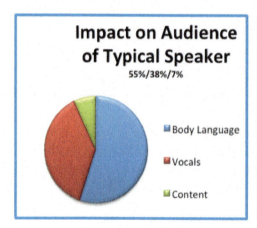

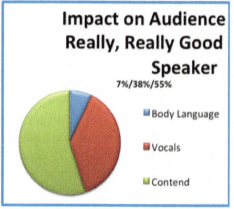

TABLE 1. Characteristics of a 55% Body Language Speaker vs. a 7% Really, Really Good Speaker

A 55%/38%/7% Speaker	A 7%/38%/55% Speaker
• Insecure	• Credible
• Unconvincing	• Authoritative
• Self-doubting	• Confident
• Soft/rushed in speech	• Speaking at a good pace and volume
• Boring	• Engaging
• Fidgety	• Moving with purpose
• Unenthusiastic and dispassionate	• Energetic and passionate

The Voice

WHAT THE SPEAKER SOUNDS LIKE

If speakers are not careful their vocal patterns can be so annoying they become distracting and cause audience disengagement even to the point where the focus moves away from the content of the speech to things like counting the number of "ahs" or "uhms."

WHAT THE SPEAKER SHOULD SOUND LIKE

1. **VOLUME** - Your speech should be loud enough to be heard at the back of the room without you shouting, which means you will need to project, to push your voice from the diaphragm. If there is any kind of noise, such as an air conditioning system suddenly kicking on, then the volume must be increased to be heard over the additional sound. In keeping the audience in mind, if you see people straining to hear what you are saying then speak more loudly; if you are not sure if people can hear you well enough then be brave enough to simple ask, "Can everyone hear me okay?"

2. **RATE** – Make sure you do not speak too slowly or too quickly and the best way to manage your rate of speed is to practice with an audio or video recorder. One thing that often happens when speakers get nervous is they tend to start speaking very quickly, in part because they want to get the speech over with so they rush. The other reason is because time travels differently when you are at the front of the room as opposed to sitting in the audience. For the speakers it sometimes feels like time has come to a slow crawl and that everything is taking a long time so they then tend to speed up to compensate.

3. **INFLECTION** – Having variety in vocal tone and pitch, meaning a sing/songy speech quality rather than a monotone sound, along with varying the emphasis of different words and syllables plus purposefully increasing or decreasing volume all creates an interesting inflection, giving the voice expressiveness. Without inflection the voice and hence the speech can sound very flat and boring.

4. **PRONUNCIATION** – Once again, when speakers get nervous vocals can be negatively affected. If English is your second language or you are from a part of the country where a different or strong dialect is prevalent, then it is very important to carefully and clearly pronounce words. If the audience can't understand you because you are not enunciating well, then you will lose them. Some students who are not accustomed to public speaking may not be aware that they have sloppy speech patterns, don't completely finish sentences, drop off the end of sentences, or tend to mumble. To learn what your particular vocals sound like, use an audio or video recorder. When you speak and people continually ask you to repeat yourself, either on the phone or in person, chances are you are not a clear speaker, but that is something that you can improve. Slow down and clearly pronounce every syllable.

5. **FILLERS** – Ever hear someone speak who continually uses the same word or couple of words over and over again, such as "uh," "er," "um," "ah," "like," "okay," or maybe they "tsk" or clear their throat? These are called verbal fillers and replace real words. Fillers are used when speakers are nervous and/or when they are searching for what to say. The best ways to avoid using fillers are to practice what you are going to say and pause just for a second or two until you find the word you are trying to think of. A brief pause is better than a filler and may take a little getting used to because as stated before, time travels differently when you are the speaker so it may feel like the pause is longer than it actually is but fillers are one of the most annoying verbal bad habits to have and one of the most important to change.

Imagine you are giving a speech and are nervous so you speak softly, quickly, with little inflection, don't pronounce your words clearly, and use lots of fillers – so what will be the audience reaction or comfort level? Your goal is to have vocals with a *positive* 38% impact, not a *negative* 38% impact.

The Body

The body language of public speaking is affected by:

- Clothing
- Stance and body movements
- Hand and arm positions
- Eye contact
- Facial expression/attitude

What the Speakers Look Like

Specifics on what to wear are discussed in another chapter, but regarding body language keep in mind that the following items are tempting to play with while speaking: open hanging sweaters, extra-long sleeves, scarves, necklaces, bracelets, rings, long earrings, strings on a hoodie, and pockets. Playing with any one of these makes you look nervous.

Hands and Arms: The following photos illustrate what NOT to do because you will look nervous, unsure of yourself, and distract from the content. These are gestures that keep 55% of the focus on body language especially when several of them are used together.

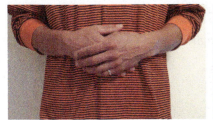
Clutching hands in front

Hands that look like a spider doing push-ups on a mirror.

The prayer, "Please let this be over soon!"

Defensiveness

Guess which hand?

Wringing ring!

Uncomfortable

Closed off - guarded

Fig leaf - feeling very vulnerable and need protection

Casual fig leaf

Holding on for dear life!

Fidgety, itchy, nervous

Hands, Face, and Eye Contact: What NOT to Do

If I let go of this sweater everything falls apart!

WHAT?!

"Like I know, right!?"

I don't know why I can't stop laughing!

It's easier if I look at the floor.

No, it's easier if I look at the ceiling.

What is everyone looking at? I know I can stare them down!

Stance: What NOT To Do

Going to trip you

Scolding position, left

Scolding position, right

Pretzel twist

Full Body: What NOT to Do, Putting It All Together

What the Speakers SHOULD Look Like

Good Body Language

- Helps audience focus on the content
- Reduces your nervousness when you know you look good and are not doing anything distracting
- Establishes confidence
- Helps fine tune body and voice behaviors

CHAPTER FOUR: What Do You Sound and Look Like When You Are Speaking?

 45

Body Language Standards

To acquire new body language skills it is necessary to first eliminate all current bad habits by learning and practicing *the top hat and bow tie* or very formal standards of public speaking and then as you become proficient at each, relax into a less formal approach. The reason why adopting a formal approach is important is because we are working toward moving from being **55%/38%/7%** speakers with 55% focus on body language, to being **7%/38%/55%** speakers with 55% focus on the speech content. The formal standards are described and depicted in photos below. Starting with a formal approach, as you will see, is like starting with a blank canvas. Some of the recommendations will feel weird at first, in fact you will not like them and until you practice them and get accustomed to their weirdness you won't appreciate their full value. If you truly keep an open mind and put these recommendations into practice then you will come to trust that you look good, relaxed, and confident and for some of you that is a big part of overcoming your fear of public speaking—so have faith in the standards!

MOVEMENT

- Do not pace. Movement should not be random because you are nervous. It should always be for a reason or purposeful and once you get to where you are going—say over to the projector screen to point something out—regain your posture and stance (explained below).

EYE CONTACT

- The standard is to look at everyone for 2 to 3 seconds, move around the room and to catch everyone (the sides too). Keep in mind that everyone likes to be included but this can be difficult because we have a dominant side and tend to focus more on either the center-to-left or center-to-right sections of the room, so looking at everyone takes some work. In addition, for some of you looking at anyone is intimidating but keep in mind that (1) everyone else in the room is going to have to give a speech too so they are apt to be very sympathetic; (2) most of the audience is thinking about their speech and how happy they are that you are up in front and they are not; and (3) establishing eye contact gives the impression that you are confident. Once you actually look at the audience you will see that they are just students like you.
- Finally, the worst advice ever given to speakers is to look over everyone's heads when you're nervous. Please do not do that, because everyone is going to know you are looking over their heads because you are nervous, plus it looks stupid! Get used to looking at your audience, not the floor, not the ceiling, not the wall at the back of the room, not the projector or computer screens, not solely at your notes or anything else. You MUST establish good eye contact to be credible, confident, and to analyze your audience during the speech.

Look at your audience

Establish eye contact
with everyone

Don't turn to face the screen
and then *forget* to turn
back to face the audience

POSTURE/STANCE/ARMS

- Posture—stand up straight, shoulders back, face forward, stomach pulled in
- Stance—feet hip-width apart and toes pointing forward
- Arms—straight down at your sides

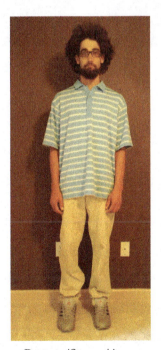

Posture/Stance/Arms

Posture/Stance/Arms

Posture/Stance/Arms

HANDS

- Hands should be used in the power zone (see the picture below)
- When in the power zone, hands are to be used for enumerating, painting a picture, or emphasizing a point. Many of you will say, "I can't help using my hands, I'm Italian!" Please note the author's last name; that is an excuse that will not fly. You can get control over your overly expressive hands with some work.

STANDARD APPROACHES FOR HANDS

Hands at side

Power Zone

Enumerating

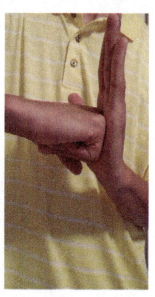
Painting a picture of a car hitting a wall

The penguin, little, flippy movements, not in the Power Zone, not powerful or confident

Facial Expression

- **Use it!** Some students who are usually very animated get up to give a speech and suddenly become totally deadpan and unexpressive. Please use appropriate facial expression to help tell your story and to give an excellent speech.

Summary

When all the standard body language approaches are incorporated into how you present yourself, you have become a mini SME, are following STATT, and used the 3Ps—all of which are helping you overcome your fears—then you are ready to be awesome. **Do this:** Walk up to the front of the room, take a deep breath, and with the mindset of a winner, trust the process, the approach, and most of all yourself. Now present a fantastic speech.

Questions for You

1. If speech content is not the main focus of an audience, then what is and why?
2. What are the various characteristics that make for strong vocal qualities of a speaker during a speech?
3. What are at least five things that students often do with body language that can be distracting?
4. What is the power zone and how is it used?
5. What are two things that you already know you will need to change based on what you have learned in this chapter, and how do you know you need to change them?

Vocal Activity

Record yourself talking to a friend and listen to your vocal patterns. Are you monotone or do you use a lot of inflection? What about the use of fillers such as "uh" or "like" or perhaps you mumble and the person you are speaking with keeps asking you to repeat what you said? Record your new insight in your journal and make a note that these are things to set as goals for feedback for your next speech.

Body Language Activity

Use your phone or a friend's phone to video record yourself practicing your speeches so you can see where you need to improve or have someone from class observe your practice and give you feedback. Do this a few times. Record in your journal where you've made improvements and the areas that you still need to work on, use the "need to improves" as the goals for your speeches. Make sure to celebrate your accomplishments!

Journal Entry:

Record your greatest learning for this chapter, what you think may be the most challenging and the easiest to accomplish. Then write some general thoughts and ideas for becoming THAT confident speaker. Go back and reread old entries. Were your challenges and accomplishments correct, if not what did you predict incorrectly that surprised you? Are some things harder or easier than originally thought?

How do you feel about the upcoming speech assignment? What are you going to make sure you do to get ready?

Recommended Assignment Appendix C- Informative Speech

CHAPTER 5

COSTUMES, PROPS, AND OTHER VISUAL AIDS

Fairlie Firari

What and What NOT to Wear

Everyone has heard the expression, "Dress for Success." Well, this applies to public speaking as well as interviewing and the workplace. Professionals, as part of audience analysis, will inquire about the environment of the participants and what is appropriate in the way of attire. Sometimes a suit is recommended, other times khaki pants or nice jeans with a dress or polo shirt are fine. Showing up to class on the day of your speech in sweats or worse, pajama bottoms, is not the way to impress your instructor or to establish credibility with your audience unless you are doing a speech related to athletics/working out or demonstrating what to wear for maximum comfort while getting eight hours of sleep, which is so very important for a college student's success.

DRESS CODE   - BY FFIRARI

It is true that most students have a limited wardrobe, but most students also have at least one interview-type outfit that they can pull together for an important speech. Regardless, at least look like you cleaned your clothes and gave some thought to your appearance—no baseball caps or winter hats, and ladies beware that you want the focus for your speech to be on your slides or your face, so do not wear provocative clothing with low-cut shirts and high-cut skirts.

It is not recommended to wear something, especially shoes, for the first time. Definitely wear clothes you have tried on and worn before so you know they are comfortable and not too tight or liable to become part of a wardrobe malfunction. As a reminder, long hair should be pulled back so it is not played with and so it does not create a distraction. Take everything out of pockets just in case you forget and put your hands in your pockets; you do not want to start jingling change or keys.

When you look good you feel good and when you feel good your confidence increases as does your self-esteem, and then your fear decreases. It is now easier to change your mindset and self-talk to convince yourself that you are a winner, that you've got this speech, and there is no reason to feel insecure. Additionally, once again the focus of the audience needs to be directed to the content you are presenting, not to a distracting piece of clothing you are wearing or a distracting behavior you are exhibiting such as flipping your hair or pulling on the tail of a scarf or sweater. And everyone please spit out the gum.

What to Bring

There are a few things you may want to consider bringing with you when giving a speech. First and foremost is an **attitude of winning and success**. This is not the first time you are reading about the need for a positive mindset, but it cannot be overstressed how important it is to approach public speaking as if an athlete going onto the field. Athletes don't approach the game by making sure the medics are ready or with a second-best attitude (that is, whatever happens, happens, no big deal). No, just the opposite, so when giving a speech try to capture and embody the attitude and mindset of a winner. Psych yourself out and tell yourself you are awesome! If you have to, fake it 'til you make it.

Notecards are important if you are using them to help you stay on track. Here are a few tips about notecards; make sure they are:

- Clearly numbered
- Bulleted without too much text so you are not tempted to read too much
- Well organized to keep you on track, contain the main points and the subpoints from your outline
- Have big enough writing so they are easy enough to read
- Written on one side only to avoid flipping back and forth
- Are in good condition, not ripped, wrinkled, or rolled up
- White, not bright red, yellow, or any other distracting color

Handout materials for the audience should be prepared in advance and there should be enough for everyone unless it is something just being passed around for show. When handing anything out timing is important. If you pass around materials while you are speaking, the audience will not focus on what you are saying, so either wait until you are finished so participants have a take-away to refer to later or do it at the beginning so participants have time to review the resources and to refocus on your speech.

You should always have some sort of **backup plan** such as a laptop and a USB in case the computer that is provided does not work. Have your presentation stored on a USB; and it is a good idea to email your presentation to yourself or to have a Prezi account that you can access in addition to the USB just in case one or the other doesn't work for some reason. Keep in mind that if you are preparing your presentation on a Mac computer you may have trouble opening it on a PC. If all else fails make sure you have a hardcopy of your presentation to refer to in case none of the equipment is working. Keep in mind that if the last option is the only option, then the audience will have a harder time following along so you will need to adapt your vocals and not lose eye contact to make sure you are super engaging to keep people interested and on the same page.

What to Show—Visual Aids

Visual aids are classified as anything used to visually enhance a speech for the support of the speaker and/or audience but should not be used in place of the speech and should be used sparingly and with purpose. In addition to showing **Power-Point or Prezi slides** there may be times when other items are appropriate to have

as **props**; for example, when demonstrating how to hula hoop you would bring a hula hoop or when demonstrating how to play an instrument you would bring the instrument. Keep in mind it is never appropriate to bring an illegal substance of any sort or a firearm or weaponry to campus or the classroom.

You as the speaker can be the visual aid especially if you are demonstrating something like parkour moves, salsa dance steps, or gymnastics so make sure you place yourself where everyone can see you. If **pictures or photos** are an important part of your presentation it might be best to take a picture of them, upload them to the computer, and insert them into your slideshow rather than to try to show them from the front of the room and risk that they will be too small to be seen from the back of the room. Again, if you hand something around for the audience to look at, then their attention will be diverted. People may start talking to each other about the prop, so you can lose control pretty quickly and then getting the group to refocus on you can be difficult. Also, be very cautious about bringing **food**, especially anything with nuts because of allergies and other potential issues with sanitation or health.

Videos or audios are often used as parts of slide presentations or as a stand-alone. Whenever possible it is a good idea to hyperlink them directly within the slides or cue them up and minimize them prior to starting your speech so that you can quickly and easily access the sites and maintain the flow of your presentation. Both should be no longer than 1 or 2 minutes when giving a relatively short speech and should be used to support, not repeat, what has been said in the speech. Good reasons to use videos and audios are to see or hear an example of what is being talked about, such as a snippet of a video of a Tough Mudder race if that is the topic. They are also good to use for added emphasis, clarity, interest, and sometimes because seeing and hearing is believing!

Why Prepare a Slideshow

What are some of the reasons it is advantageous to prepare a slideshow for a speech or a presentation?

1. For the visual members of the audience they will learn better and understand more if they can see what it is you are talking about.
2. In general, slides help everyone stay "on the same page" so to speak. When the audience is following along with you and the information on the slides, even if they take a mini-mental vacation they can quickly get back on track by looking at the slides.
3. As the speaker, slides are an excellent tool to help you stay on track which is one of the best ways to feel confident, establish and maintain credibility, and keep the audience interested and engaged.
4. Slides are used to present text, interesting graphics, charts, graphs; keep a link for videos; and overall visually enhance a speech.
5. Slides add an element of credibility and professionalism to your speech. In addition, once you have thoughtfully prepared the slide presentation you will be even more familiar and comfortable with your material. This will increase your confidence in that you know you are organized, you will be

able to stay on track and not forget what you want to say, you have important words on the slides so you will sound like a SME, and the best news of all—the audience will be looking more at your beautiful slides and less at you! All this will help lower your stress and fear.

How to Prepare a Slideshow

So integrating a slideshow into your speech, when it is appropriate, is **WHAT** you can do. Here are some more ideas on **HOW** to do it well.

1. Choose a template that is easy to read and not distracting in itself.
2. Selecting the type of font and its size and color are important in that it must be easy to read and consistent throughout; do not keep changing your font style. One or two styles at most is recommended and a large enough size to read from the back of the room, usually about size 18 to 32 for regular text and larger size for headings, 32 to 44. Figure 1 is a sample slide with a comparison of easy and hard to read font types and colors.

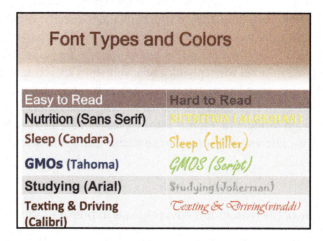

Figure 1.

3. Text on slides should be bulleted, concise, used to prompt the speaker to stay on track, and help the audience, especially the visual learners, follow along and refocus should they get temporarily distracted. Below are two slides—Figure 2 shows what not to do and Figure 3 shows what is recommended.

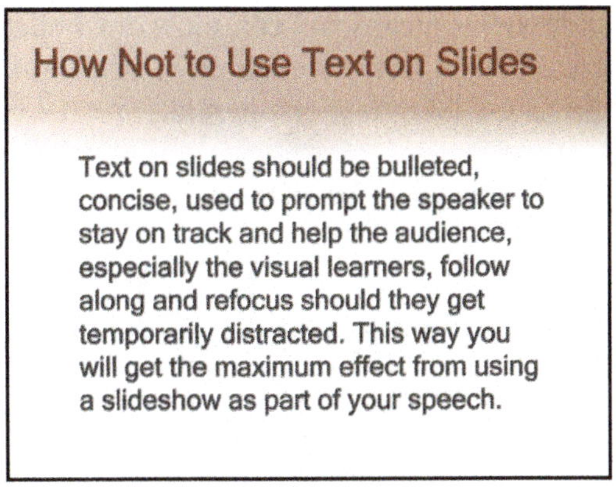

How Not to Use Text on Slides

Text on slides should be bulleted, concise, used to prompt the speaker to stay on track and help the audience, especially the visual learners, follow along and refocus should they get temporarily distracted. This way you will get the maximum effect from using a slideshow as part of your speech.

Figure 2.

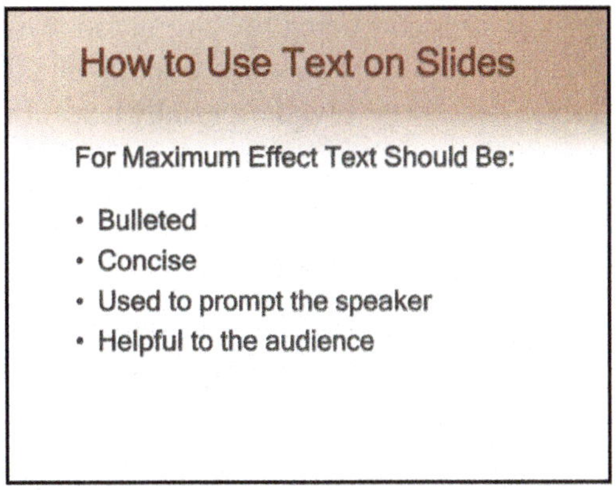

How to Use Text on Slides

For Maximum Effect Text Should Be:

- Bulleted
- Concise
- Used to prompt the speaker
- Helpful to the audience

Figure 3.

Slides with too much text tempt the audience to read ahead and since everyone reads at different rates the audience focus will be scattered. If there is a limited amount of text there is a limited amount of distraction. Additionally, too much text may tempt you as the speaker to start reading and stop speaking. Remember this is not a public reading assignment; it is a public speaking assignment. When you are reading you cannot establish good eye contact, build rapport, pay attention to how the audience is responding, and tend to become more monotone. This also applies to having too much text on your notecards.

4. There should always be plenty of what is known as "white space" on each slide so that it is easy to read and not overwhelmingly cluttered. The white space is also used to balance the slide between text and images so both are visually pleasing and have enough room on the slide. Figures 4 and 5 show the wrong and right amounts of white space and balance, respectively.

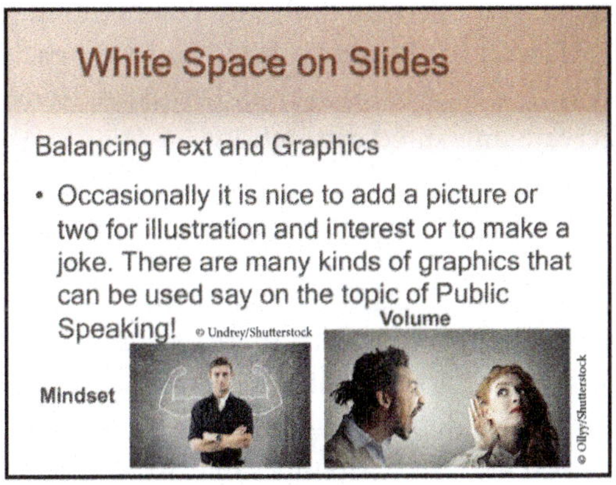

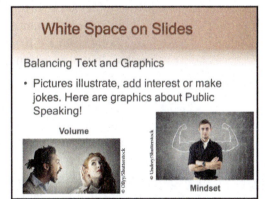

Figure 4.

Figure 5.

5. Using the animation feature of slide shows means you can show one bullet at a time, revealing only the information you want the audience to focus on. This is especially helpful when you have a lot of text on one slide.

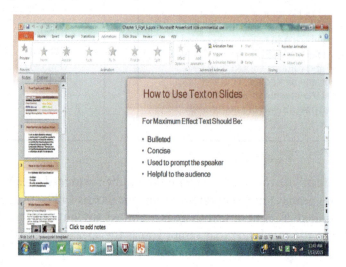

Figure 6.

Simply highlight the text you would like your audience to see first, click on "Animations" (seen at the top of the screenshot graphic in Figure 6.) if you are using PowerPoint (Prezi operates differently in that all slides are animated), and select how you would like the text to "enter," then repeat for the next bullet or graphic that you would like to reveal and so on until the entire slide is revealed. This a great way to keep tight reigns on what the audience is focused on; to hide a surprise fact, figure, or attention getter; to make a strong point; and to use if you have a lot of information on one slide and do not want the audience to read ahead. Just like with fonts and colors though, pick one style of entrance and stick with it. Do not go crazy and have each bullet point enter a different way or use a lot of bouncy and swirly options, because doing those things will create unwanted distractions.

Summary

It is important to wear the right costume for the event, which increases credibility and decreases insecurity. Using props, materials, video, audio, and slides can support your speech while increasing interest and sometimes even bringing a third dimension to your content. Finally, visual aids if not used carefully can distract from a speech but when used correctly can increase:

- Clarity/understanding
- Attentiveness/focus
- Support
- Interest
- Retention

- Credibility
- Persuasiveness

In this electronic age when most everyone has access to a computer and the Internet, it is fun and interesting to use these media to enhance a speech, especially when other types of props and materials are expensive or hard to get. Getting props, materials, and visual aids organized and ready requires the use of critical thinking and requires preparing, planning, and practicing. Practice, in particular is vital because running through your slideshow or handling props for the first time during the speech could be a disaster; working with them prior is mandatory. Keep in mind that the more you practice the better you get and the closer you are to staying within the assigned time allotment for the speech. Practice does not make perfect because perfection does not exist (doesn't that take some of the pressure off!) but it makes for really, really good and probably an A grade.

Questions for You

1. Choosing the right clothes to wear when giving a speech is important for making a good impression but dressing up or wearing a suit is not always mandatory or even the best choice sometimes. When is it appropriate to wear something else and what would you wear instead?
2. What are four things you should remember about preparing and using notecards?
3. List three visual aids and talk about the best way to use each one.
4. What do slides add to a speech?
5. What are some things you want to be careful about when using visual aids, slides, and videos as part of your speech?

Activity

Go to Ted Talks on YouTube and pick a topic of interest. Watch the entire presentation and take notes on how the presenter establishes credibility and uses pathos, logos, vocals, body language, and a presentation outline. What else do you notice that is intriguing? Do you have any advice for the speaker to make the presentation stronger? Add to your journal some things you observe that you want to make sure you do or do not do.

Journal Entry:

Record your greatest learning for this chapter, what you think may be the most challenging and the easiest to accomplish. Then write some general thoughts and ideas for becoming THAT confident speaker. Go back and reread old entries. Were your challenges and accomplishments correct, if not what did you predict incorrectly that surprised you? Are some things harder or easier than originally thought?

Recommended Assignment – Persuasive Research Paper

LISTENING AND RESPONDING

Fairlie Firari

There is a book titled, *All I Really Need to Know I Learned in Kindergarten*, but that really isn't true because we did not learn how to truly listen in kindergarten. Now don't confuse obeying and hearing with listening, which by a good description means being able to show to the person who is speaking that you have understood what he or she is thinking AND feeling from that person's perspective. Part of a very good definition was written by Thomas Lee:

> Listening is the fiber of good communication. There can be no communication without listening, and there can be no listening without genuine receptivity and a real inclination to act in response to whatever information or message is being communicated.

> Good listening is more than polite silence and attention when others speak, and it's altogether different from manipulative tactics masquerading as skill (2005).

You may be thinking to yourself right now that this is a book on public *SPEAKING* so why is listening important? There are several reasons to address listening in any book about communication but for these writings there are two in particular:

1. To listen and pay attention to audience members when they answer a polling or other type of question you ask them
2. To listen and understand questions being asked of you as the speaker

What Are the Answers to the Polling Questions?

So earlier it was stated that listening involves paying attention. Oftentimes a student will ask a polling question and then not pay any attention to the answer. For example, "How many of you know how to correctly get the fruit out of an avocado?" The answer is a show of hands of more than 75 percent of the students in the class. The speaker then says, "Okay so today I'm going to show you how." What would be a better response, given most of the class just showed they already know how to get the fruit out of the avocado? How about, "Great, so you probably know some of the same tricks I'm going to show you but you can let me know if you have any other ones, too!" Don't just ask a polling question to ask a polling question. Listen to the answer (even if the answer is a show of hands and technically not verbal), and then respond accordingly!

How Best to Respond When You Don't Get the "Right" Answer

While we are on the topic of asking questions, be careful about how you respond to an audience member when you ask a question and you do not receive the answer you are looking for, especially if the answer is correct but just not the one you want. For example, you may ask, "What is one activity you can participate in on campus that really benefits others?" Someone says, "Giving blood." You say, "Nope," because you are going to talk about signing people up for the bone marrow donor registry. WELLLLLL, think about it, giving blood is a perfectly good answer, so do not make that person wrong. A better response is, "Yes giving blood is one way and there is another way as well, which is signing up for the bone marrow registry, which I'm going to talk to you about today."

Types of Questions Asked of the Speaker and How to Respond

It is interesting to note that there are three types if questions that an audience member may ask, or three different reasons why the questions are being asked.

1. The first and simplest type of question is asked to get more information or clarification. It is a straightforward question and may require nothing more than a one- or two-word response: "How long have you been training for the Tough Mudder?" Response: "One year."

2. The second type of question is really an opinion in a question disguise and may sound something like this: "Don't you think that you should train longer than just one year before you enter the Tough Mudder?" Hmmmm, so how do you answer that question, which really isn't a question? This is a good time to use those Tier 3 critical thinking skills. So a good answer might sound like, "You are right, one year is a very short time unless the person has dedicated at least 5 to 6 hours a day to training, like I have." This way you do not make the person wrong by challenging his or her opinion and you do not risk sounding defensive with an answer like, "I have been training 5 to 6 hours a day so I know I'm ready for this challenge." This response has an implied, nah, nah, nah, nah, nah!

3. The third type of question is the hardest to handle and will probably not be something you will have to answer in a 100 or 200 level speech class but is good to be aware of, and that is the challenge question that sounds like, "What makes you the authority on the Tough Mudder since you haven't even run one yet?" At this point you want to make sure that you do not solely engage with the person asking the question and respond to the whole group. Try to respond in a way that does not sound defensive. In your mind consider the question as just a request for information and answer with something like, "I don't know yet what it is like to run the Tough Mudder

race but I'll find out on August 5th. I hope some of you will check back with me to see how I did. Thank you for your attention and I hope you learned something new about the Tough Mudder race and how it got its name." BAM! You just shut it down!

In order to determine the type of question being asked, you will truly have to listen, to understand what **and** why the person is asking such a question. Show questioners you are listening by facing them, giving them eye contact, encouraging them to speak by perhaps nodding your head a bit, and showing them that you have heard them by responding correctly.

As an audience participant it is also important that you listen to each speaker politely and attentively. It is not fair or respectful to be talking to someone else or on your cellphone when someone (including the instructor) is presenting. In fact, it is rude and distracting and you will not appreciate it if it is done to you when you are speaking. Additionally it is difficult to give feedback if you have not been paying attention. As a class you are there to help each other succeed and to become the best speakers possible in a very short amount of time, so giving good feedback is one of the best ways to help someone improve and to encourage each other.

Questions for You

1. Why is listening important if you are just speaking?
2. Because listening is a skill, it can be improved. What are at least two ways you think you can improve your ability to demonstrate that you hear and understand what is being said to you by others?
3. Showing empathy is often associated with listening. Look up the word *empathy*, define it, and then explain why empathy and listening are closely related.
4. How will you know the difference between a question asked to get information and a question disguised as an opinion?
5. What type of a question is this? "What makes you think you know so much about preparing to give a speech?" What is the first thing you would do if someone asked you this question and what would your answer be?

Activity

Watch the video of Phil Davison, GOP Candidate [Original, Full Video] by Stephen Gebhartd (5:51) on YouTube. The link is https://www.youtube.com/watch?v=djfDZ-rm9KZs

List five things Phil Davison did well and five things he should have done differently.

Journal Entry:

Record your greatest learning for this chapter, what you think may be the most challenging and the easiest to accomplish. Then write some general thoughts and ideas for becoming THAT confident speaker. Go back and reread old entries. What is getting easier for you now and what do you really need to continue to work on during your next speech? How do you feel about the upcoming speech assignment? What are you going to make sure you do to get ready?

Recommended Assignment, Appendix D–Persuasive Speech

Resources

The Twelve Dimensions of Strategic Internal Communication. Retrieved June 14, 2015. http://www.hr.com/SITEFORUM?&t=/Default/ gateway&i=1116423256281&application=story&active=no&Paren-tID=1119278064521&StoryID=1119646409453&xref=https%3A//www. google.com/

CONCLUSION

Fairlie Firari

You've Got All the Tools, Now Remember the Essentials

Here is a final recap of the main elements you need to become *THAT* confident speaker and to become a 55% content/38% positive vocals/7% body language speaker:

- **Prepare, Plan, Practice**—just like an athlete or performer, the key is the 3Ps! You must make time to prepare, plan, and practice even with a very hectic schedule, especially if you have any anxiety or fear of public speaking.
- **Become a Mini SME**—to establish credibility and confidence, one of the major fears students and speakers in general have is a lack of confidence, so you must research your topic and become an expert.
- **Use STATT**—don't ever just wing a speech or presentation, follow and trust the outline process. It is your go-to, especially if your fears are staying on track and/or remembering what you want to say when you get nervous. Use STATT and you will have them at "Hello"!

- **Create Fantastic Slideshows**—these will also help you stay on track, keep the audience engaged and in sync with your speaking points; and for those of you who do not like people looking at you—well, the focus will be on the screen and content rather than on you. Just make sure the slides are clean and well designed. Follow the guidelines in the book to make sure they do not become a distraction.
- **Dress for Success**—does it really need to be said again? You do not need to wear a suit if you do not have one but please do not show up in jammie bottoms, or with your underwear hanging out, a shirt cut down to there and skirt cut up to there, flip-flops, a hat that covers your face, a scarf or jewelry that you can't help playing with, a shirt with a remark or symbol on it that may offend someone in the audience, headphones around your neck, or gum in your mouth. Okay, there it's been said.
- **Put on the Proper Mindset**—when it is your turn to speak, take a deep breath, know that you've done everything you needed to do from the list above and that you are a winner! Like an athlete or performer ready to compete, you will approach your speech the same way! You've got this... Remember that your goal is not perfection, it is to be the best you can be which is really, really good!
- **Watch Your Language—Body and Vocals, That Is!**—fall back on the fact that you know how to stand, move, and even what to do with your hands now. Hopefully you have seen yourself on video, made some changes, and only 7% of how you influence the audience will be by your body language— don't give the audience any excuse to watch you instead of concentrating on the message. You have also practiced your vocals, received feedback, and maybe heard yourself on video; the annoying fillers are gone, your volume and rate are good so you will sound credible and ace the 35% influence on your speech.
- **Analyze, Listen, and Respond to Your Audience**—yes, *your* audience. This is your time. Find out what they know by asking polling questions and then listen and respond appropriately to their answers. The audience will feel acknowledged and a part of your speech.
- **NAIL IT!**

TIFF'S FINAL — BY FFIRARI

Follow these guidelines and keep a journal of your successes and "need to improves" and you will not only do well in this class, but you will also develop life skills that will get you through every speech and presentation you will have to do in other classes and in your professional careers. Congratulations, you are now *THAT* confident speaker—WORD!

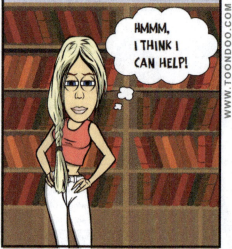

Journal Entry:

Record your greatest learning for this chapter, what you think may be the most challenging and the easiest to accomplish. Then write some general thoughts and ideas for becoming THAT confident speaker. Go back and reread old entries. Were your challenges and accomplishments correct, if not what did you predict incorrectly that surprised you? What are some of the concerns you have totally conquered? What are you celebrating most – and the end of this class does not count?! What are you always going to remember when you have to give a speech or presentation?

Recommended Assignment, Appendix E – Entertainment and/or Appendix G – Impromptu Speech

APPENDICES

Customizing for the Audience, Event, and Venue; these speech types can be used in any order and paired with any chapter.

Appendix A

- Self-Introduction and/or Elevator Speeches
  - Description and Purpose
    - This is the first time students will be in front of the group and it will be to introduce themselves in a form known as an elevator speech or a 1- to 2-minute mini-commercial about who they are and what they expect from the class. It is recommended that the instructor demonstrate how it should be done and post instructions at the back of the room.

    - The purpose is to have students give their first short speech to feel what it is like in front of the room for a relatively unintimidating assignment. This assignment will also establish a baseline.
    - The instruction in the back of the room can have bullets that say something like:
      - Your name or what you prefer to be called

- Your year in school
- What you are studying – your major
- Where you are from
- Your learning expectations for this class
- Something you would like to share about yourself that we wouldn't know

This assignment is a good starter and allows the instructor and class to start to get to know each other and gives each student some time in front of the group.

Appendix B

- Demonstration Speeches
  - Description and Purpose
    - For this speech the student will select a familiar process, action, or skill and develop a presentation to systematically explain and/or physically demonstrate how to perform the subject of the topic. It can be between 3 to 5 minutes long.
    - This is a chance to build on the baseline and gradually introduce parts of the speech format presented in Chapter 3.
  - Message Components
    - Self-introduction
    - Introduce topic to be demonstrated or explained
    - End with a recap of what was demonstrated

This assignment can show some fun and sometimes hidden talents of the students. It is an opportunity for them to be creative and not totally bound yet to a strict format.

Appendix C

- Informative Speeches
  - Description and Purpose
    - For this speech students will choose a topic that will allow them to inform the audience about something of interest to both. It should be about 6 to 8 minutes and will be developed from the information from the research paper if one was assigned.
    - An informative presentation is based on facts, includes very little if any opinion, and is given to educate, train, teach, and transfer knowledge and information.
      - Typical subjects include:
        - People
        - Programs
        - Processes or Procedures

- o Concepts
- o Events
- o Things or Objects
- o Animals
- o Places
- o It is recommended that a slide presentation is prepared.
- o STATT should be used as the format.
- o Prepare, plan, and practice.
- o Analyze the audience so that the speech is not too basic or too technical.
- o Be clear why the information being presented is of interest or beneficial to the audience.
- o Include verifiable information from the research paper and slip in a resource or two (i.e., according to the Environmental Protection Agency, the residual dust in the air around the World Trade Center after its collapse was extremely toxic and carcinogenic).
- o At the beginning of the speech, speakers can state at least two personal, self-improvement goals they hope to achieve during the speech and for which they would like to receive class feedback.
- o The students in the audience should note the goals and be prepared to give the speaker specific feedback based on those goals and based on what the focus was of the latest teaching.
- o When the speech is finished, the speaker should self-assess first, the class should share feedback next, and the instructor should comment last. Speakers, remember when you are receiving feedback you smile and say "Thank you!"

This is a good speech to videotape so students can actually see themselves and make improvements before their next major speech. Many students have a cellphone they can use if the instructor or school does not have the equipment and in fact are often willing to video a classmate as well.

Appendix D

- • Persuasive Speeches
  - o Description and Purpose
    - • For this speech students will choose a topic that they are passionate about. The speech should be about 8 to 10 minutes and will be developed from the persuasive research paper if one was assigned.
    - • A persuasive presentation is created to convince the audience to agree with the speaker's opinion and to affect change, or modify points of views or beliefs on the speaker's topic.

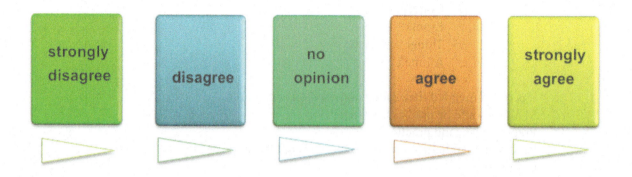

FIGURE 1. Persuasiveness Continuum

Persuasion involves moving audience opinion on the persuasiveness continuum further right than where they started before the speech was given, unless they already "strongly agreed."

- Typical subjects include (this in by no means complete):
  - People/Famous Figures/Heroes
  - Programs: Volunteer/Entertainment/Academic/Business
  - Events to Participate in or Conduct
  - Trends in Technology/Music/Sports
  - Animals in Captivity, Being Killed/Overbred or to Adopt
  - Places to Visit or Avoid
  - Laws or Rules that Should Change
  - Issues Needing Awareness: Societal/Medical/Ethical/Regarding Race, Religion, Abuse, Safety, Gender, Sexual ID
  - Theories, Some Never Proven
- It is recommended that a slide presentation is prepared.
- **STATT should be used as the format with two added important elements.**
  - **A statement explaining why this is an important topic or a thesis statement.** For example, "*Not many people know about second concussion impact syndrome so raising awareness about this condition could save someone's life.*" For a persuasive speech a thesis statement is used in addition to an attention getter, which for this topic might sound like, "*Did you know that getting a second concussion before a first concussion is completely healed usually causes death?*" (Please note that this is an actual syndrome and can cause death.)

    A thesis statement might sound like, "*There are several theories about who really shot President John F. Kennedy and today I am going to present a new idea that has recently been talked about in a documentary and that I have studied very thoroughly. I think you will be surprised at what has been discovered; it may change your mind completely on the importance of foreign government relations.*" (Please note that this is a totally made-up example.)

- **A move-to-action or reason for giving the speech.** Why is the speaker trying to persuade people to change their opinion or point of view? After the final "T" in STATT there should be a statement that instructs the audience on **what to do now.** In the case of the second concussion impact syndrome, the speaker can tell the audience to inform every athlete, coach, and parent of an athlete they know. Additionally they could join/start a campaign or put out information on social media to raise awareness.

  For the speech about the Kennedy assassination the speaker could encourage the audience to do some follow-up research on their own, ask them to read more about the new theory, and to provide the audience with links to websites or book titles where they can get additional information that will help further persuade them of the truth of the speech topic.

  The move-to-action is a *MUST* for a persuasive presentation, otherwise it is an informative speech. If the speaker cannot think of a move-to-action then the topic is not a good one for a persuasive speech because there is no persuading to do! WORD?

o Prepare, plan, and practice.
o Analyze the audience so that the speech is not too basic or too technical.
o Be clear why the information being presented is of interest or beneficial to the audience.
o Include verifiable information from the research paper and slip in a resource or two (i.e., *The American Medical Association met as recently as June 9, 2015 to address the growing concern of second concussion impact syndrome*).
o At the beginning of the speech, speakers can state at least two personal, self-improvement goals they hope to achieve during the speech and for which they would like to receive class feedback. At this point students should not be setting the same performance improvement goals as originally set. Those improvements should have been made and the bar raised to achieve higher standards, especially if they have seen themselves on video.
o The students in the audience should note the goals and be prepared to give the speaker specific feedback based on those goals and based on what the focus of the teaching was.
o When the speech is finished the speaker should self-assess first, the class should share feedback next, and the instructor should comment last. Speakers, remember when you are receiving feedback you smile and say "Thank you!"

Appendix E

- Entertaining Speeches or Speech of Choice
  - Description and Purpose
    - For this choose any type of speech that is of an entertainment or performing nature and should be 3 to 5 minutes.

      Other options might include practicing a speech required for another class and getting feedback or doing a speech over that was already done in class that you think you can now do a better job with, such as the informative or persuasive speech.

    - The purpose is to now try to relax the formal standards a little, bring more of you into the speech but still adhere to the basics as described below in order to look and feel confident and credible. Because of the often fun nature of this speech you may find new challenges such as not starting to laugh or not knowing how to respond to the audience when they laugh. On the flip side, sometimes the topics are very serious or sad so not crying or staying composed is an issue. This may seem like a simple assignment when in fact it may turn out to be one of the most difficult to conduct.

      - Typical topics include:
        - A press conference
        - An award acceptance speech
        - An award presentation speech
        - Sometimes the above two speeches are done in a pair
        - A best man or maid-of-honor toast
        - A student or faculty roast (keep it in good taste)
        - A stand-up comedy routine
        - A eulogy (speech at a funeral), some students have done their own or done one for a classmate that was tongue-in-cheek but remember it still has to be approached as a serious assignment
        - A tribute to someone in the family or someone the speaker has lost
        - A speech about an awesome pet
  - Prepare, plan, and practice—just like with every other speech, there is no cutting corners here.
  - Use relevant aspects of STATT, although they may sound more blended such as, "Good evening everyone, my name is Tiffany and I'm honored to be here today to present the prestigious coach of the year award." One sentence encompassed a nice greeting; **S for self-introduction** and **T for tell 'em what you're going to tell 'em.**

ENTERTAINMENT

Next would probably be an interesting fact about the award winner that would be the **A for attention getter:** "One thing you may not know about Coach Court is that he started out as an Art major in college and one day created a big, round sculpture that looked kind of like a basketball and the rest is history!"

Then Tiff would talk a little more about the award, which is the **T for tell 'em.** "In order to receive this award a coach must… blah, blah, blah."

This would then lead up to the actual presentation of the award which is the **T for tell 'em what you told 'em:** "So as I said a minute ago, it is my pleasure to present this award to the 2015 coach of the year."

And the wrap up, put the bow on the present-ation: "So join me in welcoming this year's recipient, our one-and-only Coach Court!"

- o Sometimes a slide show is used, believe it or not, although it is usually a relatively short one.
- o At the beginning of the speech, speakers can state at least two personal, self-improvement goals they hope to achieve during the speech and for which they would like to receive class feedback.
- o The students in the audience should note the goals and be prepared to give the speaker specific feedback based on those goals and based on what was the focus of the teaching.
- o When the speech is finished the speaker should self-assess first, the class should share feedback next, and the instructor should comment last. Speakers, remember when you are receiving feedback you smile and say "Thank you!"

Appendix F

- • Impromptu Speeches
  - o Description and Purpose
    - • For this speech each student will be given a **word/phrase** by the instructor and the student is asked to present information related to the topic whether he or she knows anything about it or not. Students will talk about whatever comes to mind when they receive their topic. It should last 2 to 3 minutes.
    - • This assignment is to evaluate how well students are able to think on their feet or to practice critical thinking skills and to use correct body language and STATT without the chance to prepare, plan, and practice but to still look like a SME.
      - • Typical subjects may be actual topics or may be fictional. The topics can be printed on a piece of paper and drawn

out of an envelope or the instructor can read from a list. Some topics used in the past include: Stinkin' Roger, Digital Moon Gazers, Pineapple Weather Predictors, Mechanical Beaver, Rogereerios

- o Trust the process and trust yourself. Don't go out-of-body, keep it together, think and be creative.
- o Use good body language and take the assignment seriously even if it is a weird sounding topic. This will earn you a lot of respect.
- o Project energy and enthusiasm about you topic.
- o STATT should be used as the format.
- o Poll the audience.
- o At the beginning of the speech, speakers can state at least two personal, self-improvement goals they hope to achieve during the speech and for which they would like to receive class feedback
- o The students in the audience should note the goals and be prepared to give the speaker specific feedback based on those goals and based on what the focus of the teaching was.
- o When the speech is finished the speaker should self-assess first, the class should share feedback next, and the instructor should comment last. Speakers, remember when you are receiving feedback you smile and say "Thank you!"

Appendix G

- • Presenting as Part of a Group – Coordination and Commitment Are Key
  - o What Is Different About Working with a Group
    - • It is up to the instructor regarding what type of presentation the groups will do—whether it is demonstration, informative, or persuasive—so this is nothing new. How the actual groups' roles and responsibilities are divided up is what is different, because now there are multiple people creating and giving the presentation.
  - o Responsibilities and Roles
    - • Each person has something unique to do for the group in the way of preparation and planning and everyone needs to come together to practice.
    - • Responsibilities can include research, writing, creative (puts the slides together), coordination (communicate and make sure project is on track), editing, logistics for practice. Persons take on the roles required for completing each of the responsibilities. Getting everyone to pull their weight and meet the deadlines can be a challenge so the coordinator needs to be confident in their role.
  - o Description and Purpose
    - • For this speech the instructor will assign the speech type and the group can select the topic; it should be 10 to 12 minutes.
  - o It is recommended that a slide presentation is prepared.

o STATT should be used as the format and it will be up to the group how to divide the presentation so everyone gets a chance to speak for about 2 to 3 minutes, to decide who will cover which parts of STATT and rotate the person who is changing the slides or the person speaking can manage their own slides. There are many different ways to divvy the workload, but keep it equitable.

o Prepare, plan, and practice

o **IMPORTANT TIP: EVEN THOUGH YOU MAY NOT BE THE ONE SPEAKING REMEMBER YOU ARE STILL PART OF A GROUP AND BEING WATCHED. KEEP YOUR BODY LANGUAGE IN CHECK, DON'T DO DISTRACTING THINGS, DON'T TALK TO ANOTHER GROUP MEMBER, AND DON'T SLOUCH IN THE BACK. PAY ATTENTION!** Such actions are disrespectful to your teammates and will negatively affect your grade.

o Analyze the audience so that the speech is not too basic or too technical. Remember the importance of listening to the responses of polling questions; and in this case, all the group members need to pay attention to the answers.

o Be clear why the information being presented is of interest or beneficial to the audience.

o Include verifiable information from the research and slip in a resource or two.

o At the beginning of the speech, speakers can state at least two personal, self-improvement goals they hope to achieve during the speech and for which they would like to receive class feedback.

o The students in the audience should note the goals and be prepared to give the speaker specific feedback based on those goals and based on what the focus of the teaching was.

o When the speech is finished the speakers should self-assess first, the class should share feedback next, and the instructor should comment last. Speakers, remember when you are receiving feedback you smile and say "Thank you!"

POSTURE — BY FFIRARI

WWW.TOONDOO.COM

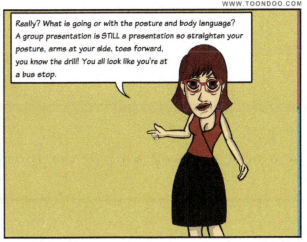

Activity – to start to coalesce as a new small group, here is an exercise you can do together:

The instructor can choose a 10-minute long (or so) video of a presidential debate. Have students break into their new small groups. Each group will be assigned one candidate to "listen" to. As the candidate speaks, identify some of the positive and negative behaviors the person exhibits and whether or not the person truly answers the questions. Is the candidate stonewalling or sidetracking? Students must listen carefully and question the answers/arguments that are offered by their candidate. The group should answer the following:

- *Topics discussed*
- *What did candidates say and do that seemed credible*
- *What did they do when they seemed to not know an answer – body language, vocals, tone of voice, etc.?*
- *Did they answer the questions instead of evade, all of the time, most of the time, some of the time, or never?*
- *What advice do you have for your candidate?*

Each group should do a short presentation about its candidate and answer the questions above.

AUTHOR BIOS

Fairlie Firari

Fairlie Firari is an Adjunct Professor at The State University of New York College at Cortland, Onondaga Community College, Syracuse, New York and Cazenovia College, Center for Career and Extended Learning, Cazenovia, but got her first teaching position at Dominican College, New York. Fairlie earned her BS at Syracuse University, S.I. Newhouse School of Public Communications and her doctorate of Philosophy in Education, Training Performance Improvement Specialization at Capella University. She has over 30 years of business experience as a program director, professional speaker, and corporate trainer. She brings close to 20 years of public speaking practice to the classroom. Along with Public Speaking Fairlie also teaches Introduction to Communication both in the classroom and online, Interpersonal, Intercultural and Business Communication, and Speech & Rhetoric. She has a training consulting business called per4mance1 and predominately conducts comprehensive career readiness program workshops. In addition to teaching, her passion is to help the hard to employ develop a professional brand and launch their career. Fairlie lives with her husband of 35 years, Bernardo Jaquez and her father Harvey Firari, an extraordinary writer and speaker. Her three beautiful children have grown and moved out, both her daughters are married and one has three gorgeous daughters of her own. In their places have moved in five, wacky re-homed dogs. You may contact her at dr.firari@yahoo.com

AnnMarie DiSiena

AnnMarie DiSiena is an Assistant Professor of Communication Studies at Dominican College in New York, where she has taught for 30 years. AnnMarie received her doctorate in Organizational Leadership with a focus in Communication Studies from Argosy University, Sarasota, Florida campus. Her research interests are in Communication Studies and Leadership. In addition to her teaching, AnnMarie serves as the Coordinator of the Communication Studies Program, the Director of Winter and Summer Sessions, and Academic Advisor for Alternative Undergraduate programs. AnnMarie has developed a curriculum and facilitated a high school public speaking program for the last seven years. AnnMarie and her family reside in Rockland County, New York. You may contact her at annmarie.disiena@dc.edu

Mark C. Meachem

Mark Meachem is an Associate Professor of Communication Studies at Dominican College in New York, where he has taught for 11 years. He received his doctorate in Educational Leadership, with a concentration on Media Studies, from Fielding Graduate University. His research interests focus on the social effects of media and online gaming. He also examines the implementation of critical thinking in the classroom. Mark is the Director of the Arts & Sciences Division at Dominican College and has worked as a newspaper reporter, a freelance magazine writer, and as an editor for *Reader's Digest*. Mark and his wife, Heather, have four sons, Riley, Cal, Aidan, and Finn. You can contact him at mark.meachem@dc.edu

Jonathan Rosen, Cartoonist for WORD.

Jonathan Rosen, former student of Dr. Firari, graduated Cum Laude from The State University of New York College at Cortland with a degree in Communication Studies in 2015. He earned multiple awards while at Cortland including; Outstanding Student Leader, 2015; Excellence in Leadership, 2015; sole recipient of the Diversity, Social Justice, and Inclusion Award, 2015; recognition for his work in Intercultural Communications, 2014; and was nominated Most Outstanding Individual Student at the Women of Color Celebration of Women symposium, 2015.

Jon aspires to work in the field of Public Relations. His dream is to work as either a storyboard revisionist or storyboard writer/creator of a cartoon show. The cartoons for this publication were inspired by his many classmates, friends and his own experience at SUNY Cortland.

CPSIA information can be obtained at www.ICGtesting.com
Printed in the USA
BVOW07s0020250815

414850BV00002B/2/P